Jane,

One idea can move you in the direction of your dreams! This book is full of them.

Love,

Colin Gilmartin

DREAM
TRAINING

To Ashley Perrin
You saw greatness in me when I couldn't see it in myself.

FOREWORD

I don't need to blame, the sins of my father, the scars of my mother – For the beast that I became. Now I shine the light on my sisters and my brothers.
Adrian Patrick, OTHERWISE

You picked up a copy of this book because you were probably curious about how a workbook could actually help you achieve your dreams. Maybe you were told to read it because something in this book will change your life for the better.

Maybe you were curious as to how so many successful people, over many generations, have used the same kinds of techniques explained in Dream Training to accomplish the seemingly impossible.

My brother Adrian and I, and our band mates, strive to better ourselves using the same lessons. With proper Dream Training, it's possible for anyone to achieve what they believe.

Adrian and I first met Colin after a show at the House of Blues in New Orleans, one of our favorite cities on Earth. While we had been a rock band for a long time, we were in the planning stages for recording our first major album "True Love Never Dies." It was shortly after the release of that album when Colin reached out to us explaining how our music had moved him to write the first edition of "Dream Training." As artists and warriors of our craft, it was wonderful to see the poet-warrior in Colin, as well. He had the same kind of fire in his eyes and intention in his heart as we did. The reason we were touring through New Orleans in the first place was to spread Light through Darkness and forge on toward our dreams.

It's funny to look back on it now and realize what he was doing with the kids he coaches. It's exactly what we try to do every night as a rock band—to inspire people of all ages to fight for what they believe in and to never give up on themselves.

Colin has assembled a book of universal truths worthy of reading at any age, but it is especially important to the youngsters growing up in today's fast-paced, social media driven world where the difference between success and failure is often hard to distinguish. We're living proof that by not giving up and working extremely hard, your dreams can come true no matter what obstacles you may face.

Ryan Patrick
Founder of 'Life by Music' – A non-profit initiative creating music & arts-based events for communities and children.

 *10% of the proceeds of Dream Training will be donated to **Life By Music***

contents

HOW TO USE THIS BOOK

INSTRUCTIONS

"Hey kid, do I have your attention? I know the way you've been livin'. Life's so reckless, tragedy endless. Welcome to the family."
Avenged Sevenfold, Rock Band

AS EASY AS ONE, TWO, THREE

ONE
If you daydream about being famous—no matter your age at this moment—let this book be your guide. It is the ultimate recyclable—like a perpetual calendar—you never throw it out because the material (like dates) is always relevant.

Right now, you are an architect looking at the blueprints for a magnificent cathedral (hint: YOU). You are like a rock musician holding the music book that contains all your secret notes. You might be an athlete in possession of the ULTIMATE playbook.

Dream Training is based on the best ideas from the greatest thinkers in the world. Let yourself become one of them.

TWO

If you are a facilitator—a Dream Training trainer—recognize you are an architect too; a project manager of sorts. The futures of the children you work with are blueprints. The worthsheets (that's right, not worksheets) in this book are self-explanatory.

Perhaps your dream is like mine—to help children become the best they can be. Abandon your fears and dive into the book with your kids—yes, go ahead and participate too. This worthbook works for everyone.

THREE

If you are a browser and have opened this worthbook at random, landing on this page, let me inform you—you picked up a super power. You hold a compilation of centuries-old, proven concepts. Want a quick demo? Smile at the person nearest you—okay, you might have to walk around to find someone.

So, what happened inside you? Feel a shift? What happened outside of you? Did the person return the smile? (Even if they didn't, you don't know how the power of that muscle contraction affected them.) When you cast a stone into a pond the entire shoreline changes. Imagine the possibilities!

THE IMPORTANCE OF DREAMS

PART ONE OF THREE

When we were little kids, many of us made capes from towels then leapt off tables and chairs. We were superheroes.

By first grade, we knew who we liked. We looked up to super-charged athletes, talented musicians, creative teachers, and courageous individuals. From firefighters to doctors, athletes to world peacekeepers, we noticed who were really good at what they did.

That's when a lot of us decided we wanted to be famous for something. Sometimes we pretended that we were just like those people we called heroes.

Can you remember HOW you felt when you played superhero? Or when you pretended to be a famous person?

_____

_____

Need help with some feeling words? Excited, energetic, brave, and courageous. Use those if they apply. See if you can come up with some of your own, too.

Can you remember WHO you looked up to when you were a little kid? WHO were the people you wanted to be like?

_____

_____

WHAT did they do?

_____

_____

WHERE did you see them?

_____

_____

WHEN did you see them?

_____

_____

WHY did you like them?

_____

_____

When we are asleep, our Dreams range from flying dogs to zombie invasions. Awake, we actively daydream about what we want in the future. "How to get the active daydreams to come true" is called **Dream Training**.

CHAPTER ONE

THE IMPORTANCE OF DREAMS
PART TWO OF THREE

When we were little kids, some of us knew what we loved to do. Some were immediately crazy for t-ball. Others sat at the piano and played around for hours without getting bored. Another group had piles of books by their beds and read with a flashlight under the covers (long after their parents said goodnight). A few began to write stories until the middle of the night. Some of us enjoyed trying different things while we looked for what kinds of activities excited us.

Did you ever notice a few kids were extremely focused on one or two things? Sometimes they chose not to come out and play because they wanted to practice, or they left the group early so they could make time to practice what they were passionate about. Various lessons took up a lot of their time.

Those kids always had lots of positive things to say about themselves and others. Sometimes they seemed already grown up. It was easy to imagine those students achieving things like becoming world-class athletes or making it big as musicians. You could imagine them as adults, wearing white lab coats and receiving prizes for science. Your parents might have even said, "He's going to go far," or "She's got talent." It might have seemed to you that those kids had a map to a fantastic future.

Those kids had the benefit of knowing what they wanted to do and knowing it would take lots of work to get to where they wanted. Yes, they had a vision, but they had people around them who showed them how to map out that plan for future success.

Most of us didn't have that "powerful knowing what we wanted" feeling in first grade, or second, or third. Even when we did enjoy something and feel strongly about making it important in our lives, we didn't know how to make a plan to be really good at that "something."

Most of us didn't have the information to switch on our "drive for fame." We were really nice little kids, we had fun, and we looked up to super-stars, but only sort-of dreamed of being one. Some of us decided that we might not be famous because there were already enough famous people in the world.

This book is already helping you think about what the word "great" means. It shows you how to make a plan to be "greater" than you are now. It gives you the information those few kids already have—If you can Dream it, you can achieve it.

You have greatness inside you. Yes, you. To unlock it you need the right tools and the right people. The words in this book combined with your words will create a map to your super-future. It's okay if you don't write in the same style as this book. The only thing that matters is that you do lots of thinking about what you want to do and, for all those things you want to do, write those things down and follow the plan.

INTERESTING STUFF ABOUT THIS BOOK

Each chapter contains questions. There are no wrong answers. Isn't that fantastic? No wrong answers.

This book contains lots of quotes about greatness. Quotes are actual words people have said.

Most chapters contain a true story about a famous person to help you see how those famous people became famous by believing in themselves.

You've already taken the first step to greatness by reading this. You've taken the second step by writing your memories from when you were a little kid.

The next step begins with recognizing you are incredibly wonderful. No one else on this planet thinks like you or does the things you do.

Dr. Seuss (Theodor Seuss Geisel) who wrote lots of children's books said: *"Today you are you! That is truer than true! There is no one alive who is you-er than you!"*

My name is _____. I am amazing. I am on the way to greatness with this Dream Training plan.

Read this aloud. Say it over and over. Say it in front of a mirror later when you are alone. Writing things and saying them are powerful ways to believe in your Dreams.

You know how Ninja Turtles or Aladdin are stories in books and movies? Well, YOU are the subject of this book. YOU are the star in a movie called your life. How fun is that? How **perfawesome** is that? Yes, perfect and awesome.

PERFAWESOME
Want to make up your own word? Take your two favorite powerful words: _____and_____. Have fun combining them into one super-word.

_____. Hey, maybe you'll become famous for that.

"Singing the song that's inside us all!" **Nothing More, Rock Band**

THE IMPORTANCE OF DREAMS
PART THREE OF THREE

Hold back nothing. There are no wrong answers.

What totally blows you away that you love to do or want to do? Something you think about lots. OR what is something you would like to have that you're not sure how to get?

_____

_____

_____

Your Dream and plan can be as simple as "I want to save up for a bike" or it might be "I want to be the scientist who discovers the cure for cancer."

Dream Training works for all Dreams. You'll go from saying I want to be the world's best "_____" to "I will be the world's best _____" to "Look out world, here comes the best _____."

Have you ever wondered how athletes, scientists, leaders, musicians and other famous people achieve their Dreams? What steps did they take?

Those people told themselves, "I will do it." They didn't say, "I might do it." They didn't say, "I want to do it." They said, "I will do it."

They said, "I AM doing it." They pictured in their minds how it would look and feel to achieve their Dreams. They did that by picturing and feeling so many times that they reworked their schedules to make their Dream come true. They didn't do it for just one thing; they used Dream Training to reach many goals.

They chose their thoughts and activities, and they hung out with people who could help them make their Dream come true. Every day they said positive things about their Dream.

They said it into mirrors.
They said it in their minds.
They said it before they went to sleep.
They said it all the time.

This kind of poem is the way Theodor Seuss Geisel wrote poems. (You know him as Dr. Seuss.) Theodor had a Dream of entertaining millions of children with his stories that sounded silly but actually had deep meaning. He created The Grinch. He created The Cat in the Hat. His belief in his talent of writing stories was so strong he never stopped believing those stories would be available to all children. Many publishers told him his work could never be enjoyed by readers. He received many rejections.

Now we wear Cat in the Hat hats, and watch The Grinch Who Stole Christmas each winter. We even write in his style (and people recognize we are writing in a Dr. Seuss way). All because he believed in himself.

All successful people in every area of life say positive things over and over. They say it because they want something and then saying it a lot helps them remember to believe it. Positive statements are called affirmations. Saying them is called affirming. Saying a positive affirmation over and over leads to success.

One of those successful people who realized their Dream of inspiring people is Napoleon Hill. He said, *"You can do it, if you believe you can."*

HOW TO BELIEVE IN YOURSELF
PART ONE OF THREE

❝ Sometimes all you need is just for somebody to believe in you in order
to be able to accomplish maybe what you never thought you could."
Andrew Brees

Andrew Christopher Brees, known to most as Drew, is an American football quarterback for the New Orleans Saints of the National Football
League. He played college football at Purdue University. Brees led the
underdog Saints to defeat the Indianapolis Colts 31–17 in Super Bowl
XLIV (the forty-fourth Super Bowl) in 2010. He tied a Super Bowl record
with thirty-two pass completions and won the Super Bowl Most Valuable
Player Award.

It was the first league championship in the Saints' franchise history.

In 2010, Brees received several awards for sports and for community
service during the reconstruction of New Orleans.

When Drew Brees received a serious shoulder injury, he could have given up and stopped believing in his Dreams. Some people told him that there was only a small chance he would play again. Drew took one day at a time. He believed in himself. He gained strength from the many people who believed in him.

How do you feel when someone believes in you?

_____

_____

Need help with feeling words? Supported, strong, capable, powerful, proud, excited, energetic, brave, and courageous. See if you can come up with some of your own.

If you believe in yourself RIGHT now, how does that feel? If you are not sure if you believe in yourself, how do you think it WILL feel?

_____

_____

Drew Brees had self-confidence.

Self-Confidence is made up of two words. Self means YOU. Confidence is that feeling of trust or belief in something or someone. It is a feeling of being certain and not being afraid or—if you are a little bit afraid—of knowing that you have the power to think about the fear and move past it.

When we know we can accomplish something, or that we're absolutely happy about trying something, then that is "self-confidence."

We can be confident in one thing and not in another. For example:

Do you know how to ride a bike? Do you hop on it without thinking about how you are going to balance?

If you can, you are skilled and confident at bike riding.

If you do not know how to ride a bike, but know that you will be able to ride after a bit of practice, you are confident.

If you do not know how to ride a bike and are afraid to try, then that does not show confidence in bike riding or wanting to ride.

Confidence is being willing to understand we might fall off the bike, but getting on it anyway.

Confidence is knowing we can ask someone to show us—and working on bike riding until we know how to ride.

Confidence is not being afraid to go after something—not being afraid of the fear.

Confidence means trusting ourselves, and feeling strong. That is the way we reach our Dreams.

Sometimes fears exist because we've heard messages from others like:

You can't do it.
You're not big enough.
You're not old enough.
You're not strong enough.
You're not capable.

Sometimes those messages are like a constant voice in our ears. Every time we wonder if something would be interesting or fun to experience, that negative voice speaks to us. And we begin believing it.

Know this: **YOU ARE ENOUGH.**

"The first duty of man is to conquer fear; he must get rid of it, he cannot act till then." **Thomas Carlyle, Philosopher**

HOW TO BELIEVE IN YOURSELF
PART TWO OF THREE

The first step in building self-confidence is OVERCOMING FEAR.

Is there something you are afraid to try?

Let's pull out a super-power you have in your brain. It's called LOGIC.
Logic is the connection and collection of REAL facts.

Count on your super-power of LOGIC to assist you in overcoming fear by asking **four questions.**

Let's use the bike example because it's a popular "something" that you probably know how to do right now. It's probably something you wanted to do when you were a little kid.

Pretend you can't ride a bike and you want to ride a bike, but you are a bit scared (not confident). Ask the **four questions**. The answers are filled in so that you can see how the **four questions** (using LOGIC) work.

1) If I do this—start to do this—what is the worst thing that could happen?

Fall off. Hurt my knee. Injure my head. Look silly to anyone who is watching. I know Joe will laugh because he's always teasing me.

2) If I do this—what is the prize—the good that comes from doing it?

I can be with my friends who know how to ride. I can get to the park faster. I can ride to school. I can be every place faster. I can get so good that I can ride BMX and do tricks. I can get a paper route and earn money.

3) Which is worse—doing this and possibly failing, OR not doing it and missing out on all the good stuff and wondering how it would have felt to succeed?

I don't want to watch everyone ride by. So what if I hurt my knee? I don't want to walk twelve blocks to school. I want to get there fast so I can hang out with my friends. And I might want to be a BMXer because I think it looks cool. Okay, I might fall off, but I can get back on. It can't be that hard. Hey, I can wear a helmet, (Joe and Steve do). I can practice on the grass at the park. I could ask someone to help me. Wow, how great it will be to have the wind in my face. The thing is my uncle Rob said that I'm a klutz. Wait! I want to try this. I don't want to miss out. It would be worse to never give it a go because of a scratched up knee. What if I fail? What if I SUCCEED! It's way worse to not give it a go.

4) What do I have to gain by doing this thing I want to do?

I'll get to school faster, so I'll have time to eat breakfast. I'll get to ride to school with some friends who already ride. Also, I just thought of something that makes me feel good: I liked helping my cousin, when he started walking, to get up and down the stairs safely. I could see myself helping him learn to ride a bike when he's older.

"As soon as you trust yourself, you will know how to live."
Johann Wolfgang von Goethe, Writer

Every time you ask these questions and move past your fear, you grow your self-confidence. Self-confidence is exactly what you need to reach your Dream.

Think of something you want to do.

I want to:

_____

1) If I do this—start to do this—what is the worst thing that could happen?

_____

_____

2) If I do this—what is the prize—the good that comes from doing it?

_____

_____

3) Which is worse—doing this and possibly failing, OR not doing it and missing out on all the good stuff and wondering how it would have felt to succeed?

_____

_____

4) What do I have to gain by doing this thing I want to do?

_____

_____

CHAPTER TWO

HOW TO BELIEVE IN YOURSELF
PART THREE OF THREE

When world famous basketball player, Michael Jordan, was cut from the High School basketball team, he said he went home, locked himself in his room, and cried.

Then he focused. He did not give up his Dream of basketball.

He did not let the coach's negative comments ruin his basketball Dream.

He loved basketball and did not want to give up. He decided to prove his coach wrong AND continue playing a sport he loved.

Michael began to say positive things about himself and his performance. He began to believe those things he said. Soon he could picture himself as a skilled player. Soon he could imagine how it would feel to be successful. He worked hard on his skills and kept thinking those positive thoughts.

"Always turn a negative situation into a positive situation." **Michael Jordan**

At the end of this book, you'll find a list of famous people who changed the world. They told themselves over and over that they could do the things they wanted to do.

The word we use to tell ourselves we can do something is affirmation.

Using positive affirmations can help you build self-confidence by changing your thoughts.

When the thought of: "I don't have" or "I can't" or "It's never been done before" enters your mind, change the thought to "I will have" or "I can" or "I'll be the first to…"

I **AM** affirmations work well. Example: I **AM** enjoying practice and will be the best soccer player…

Five steps to follow when creating an affirmation: be positive, focus on the now, be yourself, write/speak/interact with passion, don't worry about HOW things will happen (simply believe they will), and repeat the affirmation.

Example of a positive affirmation:

I AM using my magnificent mind to make my Dream happen.

Let's build one for the purpose of working through this book.

I AM using my amazing mind to work through this book.

I AM excited that this book will show me how to reach my Dreams.

"I am the greatest. I said that even before I knew I was." **Muhammad Ali, Athlete.**

Use the one above or create one of your own here:

Your thoughts are the seeds that will grow into fantastic achievements.

Autosuggestion means to hold a thought in your mind and to concentrate on that thought. An example of autosuggestion is to repeat to yourself the affirmation you created.

Let's look at the power of autosuggestion.

Imagine if a little kid repeated this message to himself or herself: **I have no balance — I'll never ride a bike.** Do you think that kid will ever ride a bike? If they do learn, can you imagine how long it would take? Can you picture how scared they might be every time they have to negotiate a corner?

Now imagine that same person repeating: **I AM the best bike-riding student ever — I AM excited to ride to school.** Do you think that person will ever ride a bike?

Would the world know about Drew Brees or Michael Jordan if they had chosen to repeat the negatives they heard from others?

When we say something over and over it becomes real. It's a natural law.

"Greatness is the ability to recognize the power of your own mind, to embrace it and use it." **Napoleon Hill, Author**

MENTORS
PART ONE OF THREE

"*It is only from the people I've had the good fortune to meet that I am learning the lessons to guide me.***" Simon Sinek, Author**

No one can become truly great without help. To be successful, you'll need the help of others along the way. All successful people looked up to someone else's example (and often continue to do so).

Mentors are people who inspire, support, and lead us. They are sometimes called our inspirational advisors.

What does inspiration mean? Who are advisors?

Inspiration means motivation and encouragement.

People who share their experiences and are willing to help us feel and be our best are called inspirers, advisors, or mentors. We can be inspired through books, films, and face-to-face meetings.

Michael Jordan worked hard after he'd been cut from the basketball team at school. He believed in himself, he had passion for the sport, and he found inspiring people to help him reach his goals. He went on to play basketball in college.

"Other than my parents, no one had a bigger influence on my life than Coach Smith. He was more than a coach — he was my mentor, my teacher, my second father. Coach was always there for me whenever I needed him and I loved him for it. In teaching me the game of basketball, he taught me about life." **Michael Jordan**

Once you have your affirmation, or affirmations, it's time to look around for people who have experience in greatness. You can tap into their excellence as if it were your own. You can achieve much more when you have one or more people advising and guiding you.

MENTORS
PART TWO OF THREE

Remember the bike-riding example?

If you don't know how to ride a bike, who is a good bike rider that you know?

When you see them ride, do you want to ride like them? Do you like their style?

If you do ride a bike, can you remember when you didn't know how? Who did you look up to who did ride a bike?

If you do ride a bike, is there anyone who looks up to you who you could show how to ride a bike?

Isn't it interesting that while people inspire you, you are probably inspiring others?

Remember the Dream you identified—the "something" you want to do (like become a football player, doctor, musician)?

Do you have some ideas of who can help you reach that Dream? They can be people you already know or they can be people you never meet in person but know about their accomplishments.

People in my life right now:

_____

_____

People I have read about or heard about:

_____

_____

MENTORS

PART THREE OF THREE

Look for these qualities in your advisors, mentors, and inspirers:

1) Dependability – Can you count on them to show up? Who is someone you can depend on in your life? What makes them dependable?

---

2) Loyalty – This means being faithful. Loyal people are honest and positive with their words. When they show up, they appear to be filled with a caring quality that makes you feel their true kindness and respect. We say that soldiers are loyal to their country. Doctors are loyal to their patients. To whom or what are you loyal?

---

3) Ability – This means being sensible, skillful and intelligent. What qualities do you already possess that will help you reach your Dream?

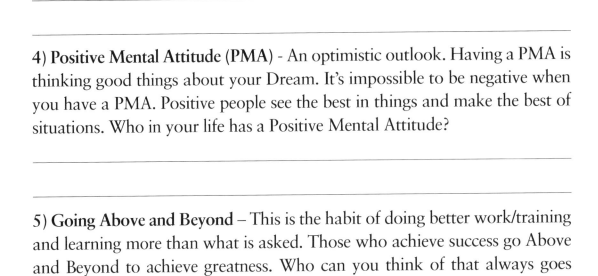

4) Positive Mental Attitude (PMA) - An optimistic outlook. Having a PMA is thinking good things about your Dream. It's impossible to be negative when you have a PMA. Positive people see the best in things and make the best of situations. Who in your life has a Positive Mental Attitude?

5) Going Above and Beyond – This is the habit of doing better work/training and learning more than what is asked. Those who achieve success go Above and Beyond to achieve greatness. Who can you think of that always goes Above and Beyond what they are required to do? How do they go Above and Beyond?

6) Faith – This is a strong belief in things (even things that cannot be seen). Believing you can do something you have never tried before requires a strong faith. Think about all of the people in your life. Which of those people are believers in greatness? Who demonstrates that faith in themselves? Have they shown they have a belief in you?

"Faith is the ability to see the invisible and believe in the incredible and that is what enables believers to receive what the masses think is impossible."
Clarence Smithison, Author

If you have a Dream, feel confident about yourself and your plan, and engage others in your life who share your energy about that plan, you are moving in the right direction.

"I don't believe that that little word 'can't' should stop you. If you don't have the right experience to reach your goal, look for another way in."

Richard Branson, Businessman

When we make our DREAM, create an affirmation, and then get it working for us by repeating it, we will find people who want to support us in reaching our Dreams.

"I try to be a guide for people, to make their darkness bright and to make the pathway light, and never to condemn or control or criticize."
Little Richard, Songwriter

Famous people have mentors before they reach fame and during the time they are famous. They see qualities in another and aim to reach those heights of achievement or surpass them. But never in a competitive "I have to beat that person" way, rather in a joyful "I love what this person stands for" way.

As for my band, well, my mentors were Duke Ellington, Benny Goodman, Jimmie Lunceford, and no one had a band more smartly dressed than Duke.
B.B. King, Iconic Musician

"I want to show you a better way, so you and I will finally be free! Won't you please take this?"
Gemini Syndrome, Rock Band

CHAPTER FOUR

SOUL POWER
PART ONE OF THREE

You might hear people talking about the "heart and soul" of the matter or doing something from the "heart and soul." This is an expression meaning to do something with strong, caring emotion.

The **heart** is a muscle in our body—the pump that keeps our blood flowing.

But what is the soul? The early Greeks called the soul "the heart of hearts."

The **soul** is not a physical body part. It is a word that captures all the non-physical (the non-body) parts of us. We sometimes call this the essence.

To give you an example of soul: If your body is a light bulb, then your soul is the electricity.

Most people believe that every living creature and plant and even everything has a soul. That's because everything has a meaning and a purpose — an inner identity — an essence. A reason for being.

For example, a piece of music made up of notes that were written to be played together by a composer brings something soothing or magical to your ear. Therefore it has a purpose—its soul.

In a person the soul is much the same—it has a purpose, something magical that you might imagine is like a "live" identity inside you.

It can be said that the best part of us cannot be seen. What is meant by that is the deepest thoughts and kindest intentions begin inside each of us in our heart of hearts, in the soul. The actions we take based on those thoughts are "seen" in ways like people feeling good from receiving the outcomes of soul power. These could include using an invention to improve their life (which was created from original deep thoughts), or listening to music that was created through soul power, or reading a book created from someone's heart of hearts.

When you decide to go after a Dream, you can move toward it with a determination that includes all your thinking power, all your physical energy, and the drive from your soul. We call that Soul Power. Soul Power is an attitude that puts Dreaming into action.

"The biggest adventure you can take is to live the life of your Dreams."
Oprah Winfrey, Inspirer, TV Personality, Philanthropist.

Here is a list of people who overcame all kinds of barriers to achieve success. They used positive affirmations, they repeated those affirmations, they were inspired by others, and they had self-confidence. They used Soul Power to achieve their Dreams.

Choose a few people from the list. Look them up (research) to find out how they overcame difficulties and realized their Dreams.

IF THEY CAN DO IT, SO CAN YOU!

Muhammad Ali

Joan of Arc

Richard Branson

Drew Brees

Andrew Carnegie

Mark Cuban

Thomas Edison

Napoleon Hill

Thomas Jefferson

Helen Keller

Will Smith

Hope Solo

Booker T Washington

George Washington

Lionel Messi

Lil Wayne

Ralph Waldo Emerson

Abraham Lincoln

Jackie Robinson

LeBron James

CHAPTER FOUR

SOUL POWER
PART TWO OF THREE

Soul Power feels like a "burning desire."
Seven things make up **Soul Power.**

ONE: Have a Dream
You need to know what you want to achieve (a Dream or Dreams) and what you are willing to do in order to achieve that Dream or Dreams.

It's important to write down your Dreams.

Remember—Dream Training works on all Dreams. It takes the same positive attitude to become an athlete or a doctor.

Do one thing every day that brings you closer to your Dream.

"In this life there's no surrender
There's nothing left for us to do
Find the strength to see this through" **Otherwise, Rock Band**

TWO: Have an Affirmation

Did you create one in the earlier chapter? Rewrite it here or make a new one.

A powerful start to an affirmation is "I AM." Example: I AM excited about learning DREAM TRAINING.

_____

_____

Repeat your affirmation EVERY morning after you wake up and EVERY evening before you go to sleep. Say it in front of a mirror.

Once you begin imagining yourself with your Dream, knowing how it will feel, you will line up the necessary work, and any doubts you may have had will fade away.

"Visualization is the great secret of success."
Genevieve Behrend, Author

THREE: Positive Mental Attitude

Positive Mental Attitude is a crucial part of Soul Power. It is important to have a PMA because this will determine how and when you achieve your Dream.

Your attitude is reflected in every word you speak, and your attitude is louder and more powerful than any spoken words. Your attitude is the total of your thoughts, feelings, and behavior at all times.

FOUR: Adversity

Your Soul Power will be tested many times. No one can achieve "greatness" without being tested by tough times.

Every difficult time or exercise brings with it a promise of opportunity.

Temporary defeat **IS NOT** failure unless you accept it as failure. Don't quit on your Dream before the miracle happens.

"I've failed over and over and over again in my life and that is why I succeed."
Michael Jordan

Has there ever been a time when you were going through a difficult time (facing adversity) and then learned something new because of it?

What was the adversity? What did you learn?

FIVE: Mentors
MENTORS are individuals who inspire.

If you have not already identified your inspirational advisors, return to chapter 3 for a reminder. Keep your mind open for guidance from within.

SIX: Understanding Your Soul Power
The soul is the engine of life. Remember, it's like if your body is a light bulb, the soul is the electricity. If your heart is the pump, the soul is the engine. When we put our positive attitude into action, it's called **Soul Power**.

Infinite means never-ending. Intelligence means knowing things.

It's important to recognize that there is an Infinite Intelligence all around us. The universe in which we live has an order of which you are an integral part.

You are **Infinite Intelligence.**

"Your power of thought is the only thing that you have complete, unchallengeable control over. You do this through the power of will."
Napoleon Hill, Author

SOUL POWER

PART THREE OF THREE

A ction Beyond Paper

You can share your Soul Power with someone around you.

Write a note to someone who always influences you to do the right thing or helps you achieve your Dream.

Thank them for doing what they do.

Want some help with the words?

Dear _____,
Thank you for helping me _____. It's so good of you to take the time to _____. I know that your input will help me reach my goals.
Sincerely, _____.

"Make it a habit to tell people thank you. To express your appreciation, sincerely and without the expectation of anything in return… Truly appreciate life, and you'll find that you have more of it."
Ralph Marston, American Writer

DEVELOPING THE TRAINING HABIT
PART ONE OF THREE

"You miss 100% of the shots you don't take."
Wayne Gretzky, Hockey Player

Willpower means being determined.
When someone has strong willpower, it means he or she can control his or her behaviors and emotions (actions and feelings).

It is important to develop willpower to reach your Dream. Creating strong willpower is like creating strong muscles. People have to work out and train themselves to be stronger.

The way to get strong willpower is to develop habits and become better at concentrating.
It is having a mindset of "I will" and "I can."

Habits are behaviors that we get used to doing and then continue to do them a lot.

Some people are always late. They might not be organized and always leave their shoes in a different place and spend time looking for them when it's time to leave the house. They may not set their alarm clocks regularly and so forget to set the clock when they have morning appointments. Being late is a result of not having efficient habits.

Some people are on time. They always put their shoes in the same place so they never have to look around for them. Leaving their shoes in the same place is a habit. They have a routine to set their alarm clocks so that they are always awake in time to make it to a morning appointment. Setting their alarm clocks is a habit.

Power of Habit

Habits are powerful because you don't even have to think about them, you just do them.
When you decide to make something a habit, you have to practice first. When it becomes a part of what you do (a natural feeling), it frees up space in your brain to focus on other things.

Habits can be negative too. Biting nails can become a habit.

Developing a good habit starts with a psychological pattern called a "habit loop."
Many will say it's difficult to establish a habit or break one, but if you want something to start or stop, a "habit loop" is as easy as ABC.

A ACTION

There will be a sign that initiates the behavior. Just like a movie director calls ACTION, bring your mind to "see" what's in front of your camera—your eyes.

Example of starting a habit to save for a bike. Every time you see someone riding a bike, you know you have to have one and promise yourself you'll save for one. ACTION! Picture yourself buying one. Every time

CHAPTER FIVE | **DEVELOPING THE TRAINING HABIT**

you receive money, ACTION! Imagine a photograph of you buying your bike.

Example of stopping a habit of eating junk. Get a clear picture in your head of the benefits of not eating junk (better performance in school, feeling better about your body, increased speed at track, less stomach aches, clearer mind—whatever it looks like to you). Whenever you are in the situation that makes you want junk food, know that your inner director will show up. ACTION! Show yourself the "better you" photo in your head.

B BUSINESS

The business of being busy doing what your new habit needs you to do. As soon as you've taken ACTION in picturing the habit you want to create or break, make it your business to busy yourself.

Bike example: ACTION — you've got that picture in your head. Now, attach some business to it. Work an extra hour. Stop picking up a slush drink on the way home from school and save that money. Make it a business that supports the ACTION.

C CONGRATULATE AND COMPENSATE

In the habit loop, when you've taken ACTION and done the BUSINESS, then you can CONGRATULATE and COMPENSATE yourself.

With the example of saving for a bike and therefore getting out of the habit of buying slushies or getting into the habit of working an extra hour, you can find something that makes you feel good. It could be as simple as congratulating yourself (while looking into the mirror) or it could be making yourself a slushy in the blender at home.

Coaching mentor Jeff Tipping says, "First you make your habits, then your habits make you."

That means you choose the behavior you want to become natural, and then that natural behavior makes you a better bike rider, athlete, student, musician.

Can you think of any habits you have formed?

_____

_____

Do you have any habits you would like to replace with new habits to help you reach your Dream?

_____

_____

_____

"Motivation is what gets you started. Habit is what keeps you going."
Jim Ryun, Athlete

DEVELOPING THE TRAINING HABIT
PART TWO OF THREE

How to Change a Habit

Start simple

Pick one habit. Don't rush it. Let's say eventually you'd like to practice two hours a day at something new. Make the first step thirty minutes. Build on it over time. Tiny steps toward your goal can be increased once the habit is developed.

Change your surroundings

This is the easiest way to change your behavior because you will not be around a place that has the old signals. Changing the environment breaks up old patterns.

Let's say you want to have better grades. You might want to sit at your desk at home and not near the television where you usually bring your schoolwork. By removing the signal—sitting on the couch near the TV—

you change it up and do not turn on that TV because you're not there.

Are there any changes to your routine that you can take advantage of? For example, is there the start of a new practice schedule or a change of season that could shake up your routine so you can insert something new?

Commit to one month
Three to four weeks is all the time you need to make a habit automatic. After a month, the new habit becomes much easier to maintain.

Do it daily
Consistency (a regular schedule) is critical if you want to make a habit stick. If you want to start exercising, go to the same gym every day at the same time for your first thirty days.

It's more difficult to develop the habit if you only go twice a week.

Set reminders
Tape a note to your mirror. Put another in the bathroom. Send yourself scheduled e-cards or messages on your phone.

Replace negatives with positives
If the habit you want to develop means you have to give up something, or the habit is to give up something, get creative and find a replacement for what you are giving up. Let's say you want to stop eating donuts. Make sure you have something healthy planned and available at the time you'd usually reach for the donut. Or if you are planning to cut back on video games, replace them with something related to your Dream that will still give you some stimulation, like reading about things related to your Dream.

Keep going

If you accidentally forget one day, don't beat yourself up over it. Just keep going. Remind yourself with an affirmation "I AM working at developing this habit until I master it."

Surround yourself with role models

Spend time with people who already have the habits you want to develop.

Use Autosuggestion

When you repeat affirmations, you harness the power of language to support your Dreams. That builds self-confidence and develops positive habits.

"It's the repetition of affirmations that leads to belief. And once that belief becomes a deep conviction, things begin to happen."
Muhammad Ali, Athlete

Visualize your benefits and stay enthusiastic!

Visualize all the ways this change (your new habit) is going to affect you positively. Don't forget, this is exciting! Throw your energy at it. The more positive you are, the stronger you'll become.

DEVELOPING THE TRAINING HABIT

PART THREE OF THREE

The Power of Concentration

Concentration is when you can focus on one thing while blocking other distractions.

Have you ever watched what happens when you hold a magnifying glass over a piece of paper on a sunny day? If not, you could ask someone to try it in a safe location.

When the rays of the sun are focused on a single spot of paper (through the glass) the heat is concentrated on the paper and begins to brown, smoke, or even catch fire.

Concentrate the sunlight and you get action. Scatter the light and it doesn't set anything on fire.

Your power of concentration works the same way. When you focus your thoughts, you get extraordinary results. Scatter them and not much happens (toward your Dream).

When you are able to set your concentration to one thing, and focus on it with your whole heart, mind, and body, your journey toward greatness begins.

DEVELOPING YOUR POWER OF CONCENTRATION

1. Decide on what you want to concentrate

It's easy to become busy with activities for school and after school. As you get older, you have more responsibilities.

The best thing to do is stop and take a deep breath then pick one task. Set everything else aside. If you have trouble getting the other "things" out of your head, write them down on a list so that you are free to forget them for the time you are working on one thing.

You will find that you will accomplish more if you are focused on one task at a time.

2. Avoid constant invasions of your senses

Multi-tasking (doing more than one thing at a time), loud noises, and visual stimulation (from television, texting or video games) make concentration difficult. Being around these things can put you into a habit of non-attention. That habit can be hard to break.

3. Make it a point to put your full concentration on whatever you are doing

Be present in your day-to-day life, whether you are eating, visiting a friend, exercising at the gym, or riding your bike. Focus on what is happening in the moment. Taste your food. Listen to your friend. Feel your muscles strain. Look at your surroundings.

4. Stay calm

Deep concentration works when you calmly focus on an activity.

"You don't have to slow down, just calm down."
Bob Proctor, Motivational Speaker

5. Take breaks.
Go outside and breathe deeply or take a brisk walk. Make yourself do this often and you'll be able to return recharged and ready to focus creatively.

6. Learn to meditate.
Meditation is the most powerful of all concentration techniques. For as long as there have been people, there has been meditation. Your road to greatness will be much clearer if you meditate at least five minutes daily.

Benefits of Meditation: Improved health, less stress, fewer negative feelings. An overall feeling of safety, wellness, and connection to yourself and to the world.

When you meditate, you might feel a connection to another part of yourself. It might feel kind of like you are meeting someone who is a part of you who knows more than the regular you. This is called your higher self.

How to Meditate
There are many ways to meditate, but they all include calm breathing and quiet concentration.

Heart Meditation

Step 1: Heart Focus
Focus your attention on the area around your heart, the area in the center of your chest.
If you prefer, the first couple of times you try it, place your hand over the center of your chest to help keep your attention in the heart area.

Step 2: Heart Breathing
Breathe deeply and imagine that your breath is coming in and going out through your heart area. Continue breathing with ease until you find a

natural inner rhythm that feels good to you.

Step 3: Heart Feeling

As you maintain your heart focus and heart breathing, recall a time when you felt good inside. Let that remembering bring goodness to you.

One of the easiest ways to generate a positive, heart-based feeling is to remember a special place you've been or the love you feel for a close friend, family member, or treasured pet.

You can do the Heart Breathing Technique anytime, anywhere, and no one will know you're doing it. In less than a minute, it creates positive changes in your heart rhythms. This sends powerful signals to your brain.

Try this one minute before school and another minute before you go to bed. Do it any time you are in a difficult situation. The more you do it, the more you'll feel calm when you're not doing it. Soon that state of mind will be a regular part of your day.

GOING ABOVE AND BEYOND
PART ONE OF THREE

❝*People of excellence go the extra mile to do what's right.***❞**
Joel Osteen, Author

Going Above and Beyond means doing a better job than what has been requested.

Going Above and Beyond will make you stand out from others. People will remember you. You will also become more fulfilled.

To get to the top, you have to be willing to do more than you're asked to do and do it with a great attitude.

I was once training a group of kids during summer camp. One day I noticed a young boy stayed after camp to put in more time soccer training. He became so involved in his "going Above and Beyond" that his mom had to call him three times before he heard her say it was time to leave. He looked up and said to her, "Mom, I'm going the extra mile!"

You can go Above and Beyond anytime in any activity and no one needs to tell you to do it. That's how all the famous athletes, musicians, and other successful people do it.

A way to get into the habit of going Above and Beyond is to be of service to others. All truly great people know that serving others has great rewards.

"The best way to find yourself is to lose yourself in the service of others."
Mahatma Gandhi, Activist, Philosopher

Giving does not refer to giving money or donating toys. The easiest ways to go Above and Beyond are simple gestures: a smile, a compliment, opening a door for someone, or saying hello.

A smile? Yes. Suppose you see the bus driver every day, flash your bus pass, and take a seat as your regular routine. Going Above and Beyond is easy and rewarding in this case. Simply add a smile or a "good morning/afternoon" or a "thank you" when you get off. That is going Above and Beyond what you usually do. It changes stuff inside you, and it changes stuff inside the driver. Therefore a ripple effect (like throwing a pebble into a lake) takes place.

You do not have to search out people to be of service to. Just do things for the people around you, including your friends and family.

"Service to others is the rent you pay for your room here on Earth."
Muhammad Ali, Athlete

Make a list of people you could be of service to and write down what you could do to serve them.

CHAPTER SIX | **GOING ABOVE AND BEYOND**

GOING ABOVE AND BEYOND
PART TWO OF THREE

Humility is a word that means kindness and quietness. You might hear it called "modesty." It is the opposite of being a big shot who announces everything he or she does (for attention).

Humility is a character trait you will discover in yourself when you are of service to others.

CONFUSION: There is a word similar to humility that is called humiliation. It is not related to humility. Humiliation means to think less of someone or yourself and to do things and say things that demonstrate you think less.

Humility is thinking of others more. It means being unselfish.

Affirmation Today, I will be of service to the people around me.

"You are what you do, not what you say you'll do." **C.G. Jung** Psychologist

After you go Above and Beyond, you will notice interesting opportunities come your way. This is one of the benefits of going Above and Beyond.

A PROFILE OF SUCCESS:

Booker T. Washington was born during the time when America allowed slave labor.

Booker was born on April 5, 1856. His parents were held as slaves and so he himself was born into slavery. At that time, it was illegal for anyone to teach slaves to read and write. At sixteen years old, he left home and walked five hundred miles with only the hope of getting an education.

Booker T. went Above and Beyond everyone's expectations. He became an educator, author, speaker, leader in the African-American community, and an advisor to presidents of the United States.

"I have learned that success is to be measured not so much by the position that one has reached in life as by the obstacles which he has overcome while trying to succeed."
Booker T Washington, Educator

GOING ABOVE AND BEYOND
PART THREE OF THREE

Has there been a time when you have gone Above and Beyond? (Remember, this means without expecting anything in return.)

_____

_____

_____

_____

Action Beyond Paper

Here's your opportunity. Choose two or three. Or do one several times for different people. When you've done some of these things, don't stop, but be sure to make a few notes to record how it felt.

Smile at someone you see.
Pick up some trash.

Greet someone you haven't greeted before.

Pay a genuine compliment to someone.

Help a person carry his or her groceries.

Read to a younger child.

Volunteer to work at a food pantry, soup kitchen or local animal shelter.

Stay after school to help a friend work on his or her Dream.

Organize a food collection for the local food bank.

Volunteer to teach a younger child to play a sport.

Offer to run an errand.

After a regular chore, add another action (like wiping counters after the dishes).

Clean something in your home without being asked.

CHAPTER SEVEN
POSITIVE MENTAL ATTITUDE
PART ONE OF THREE

❝*The greatest discovery of my generation is that a human being can alter his life by altering his attitudes.*❞
William James, Psychologist

Positive Mental Attitude means a confident and optimistic way to think and feel.

How do you feel most of the time? Are you happy, excited, and enthusiastic? Do you smile a lot? Do you like to laugh? How do you feel about these areas of your life: where you live, the school you go to, the activities that you participate in, the community that you live in, the city that you live in? Use the space below to describe your feelings about all of these categories.

Most of the time I feel:

Do I smile and laugh a lot?

_____

I feel this way about where I live:

_____

I feel this way about where I go to school:

_____

I feel this way about my community and my city:

_____

I feel this way about my activities:

_____

"I am focused on what I am after, the key to the next open chapter 'cause I found a way to steal the sun from the sky. Long live that day that I decided to fly from the inside."
Shinedown, Rock Band

POSITIVE MENTAL ATTITUDE
PART TWO OF THREE

Flying from the inside: More ways to develop a Positive Mental Attitude

1. Picture yourself already having reached your Dreams and Goals
Write down your Dream. Read it to yourself lots of times.

2. Supersize your Positive
Put up pictures of anything and anyone to remind you of your Dream. Those images will "rub off" on you.

3. Focus your attention on the "Can Do" part of every difficult situation
If something seems overwhelming, break it up into smaller, manageable tasks.

4. Learn to change the "unpleasant" into opportunity
Immediately get extra help to change it the next time.

5. Go out of your way to praise good qualities in others

Nothing is more rewarding than being kind, courteous, and complimentary.

6. Great achievers have role models

Find your role model's qualities online at www.Iamdreamtraining.com. Can't find your hero online? Let us help you develop their profile.

7. Remember that affirmations work.

Chicago businessman William Clement Stone would say, "I feel healthy, I feel happy, I feel terrific!" And guess what? He did.

Affirmation I am so happy and grateful now that I am unstoppable.

CREATE YOUR OWN POSITIVE ENVIRONMENT

Now it is time to create your own environment of the great by putting up pictures that inspire you.

Pictures and quotes from this book and many others will help keep you focused, energized, and ready for your journey of achievement.

Writing about positive places and people generates enthusiasm. What places do you feel positive? Where do you enjoy being?

_____

_____

_____

_____

THOUGHTS ARE THINGS
"I hold it true that thoughts are things;
They're endowed with bodies and breath and wings:
And that we send them forth to fill
The world with good results, or ill.

That which we call our secret thought
Speeds forth to earth's remotest spot,
Leaving its blessings or its woes
Like tracks behind it as it goes.
We build our future by thought,
For good or ill, yet know it not.
Yet so the universe was wrought.
Thought is another name for fate;
Choose then thy destiny and wait,
For love brings love and hate brings hate."
Henry Van Dyke, Author

Begin to understand—believe that "thoughts" are things.

POSITIVE MENTAL ATTITUDE
PART THREE OF THREE

Dream + Desire + Devotion = Greatness!

Which means:

What you want to do + Really wanting to do it + Your throwing all your skills at getting it = GREATNESS

You come into this world with a little bit of your birth mom and your birth dad plus all of their parents inside you. This history, plus whatever you experience from the time you're born (like whom you live with, where you live, what food you eat, and other stuff) puts you where you are now.

It's like building a house. You have the foundation (the family history), and then as you move along in life, you start putting up the walls and designing the rooms. And the great thing is, you get to choose your Dream and how you will achieve it.

"Everything can be taken from a person but one thing: The last of human freedoms — To choose one's attitude, In any given set of circumstances."
Victor Frankl, Holocost Survivor, Author

PROFILE OF PERSONAL SUCCESS:

You've probably heard of actress Hilary Ann Swank. Hilary was born in Lincoln, Nebraska, and by the time she was six, her father, had moved the family to Bellingham, Washington. Hilary and her parents lived in a trailer park near the edge of the city. Many of the kids in her class were mean to Hilary because she was poor. She didn't have the clothes they had and didn't live in a fancy house.

Hilary spent a lot of time on her own (not hanging out with kids from school). She read lots of books and watched movies. She understood the struggles of the characters in stories because she had her own struggles.

Hilary discovered how she could overcome her life of being poor by reading, watching films, and taking examples from some of the heroes in those stories.

Hilary's mother talked to Hilary about self-confidence. After that, Hilary discovered acting. One of her first performances was in fifth grade. The class put on the play The Jungle Book. Hilary was chosen to play the little boy who had been raised by wolves—the man-cub, Mowgli. At first, she wondered if she could act the part of a young boy, but the challenge excited her.

Hilary did a great job. Her mother supported her in joining a theatre group where she received the Best Junior Actress Award at the Bellingham Theatre Guild.

The more Hilary succeeded, the more confidence she developed. She began working hard at swimming and gymnastics. As a teenager she competed in the Junior Olympics as a swimmer. By age sixteen, she made the decision to pursue acting as her main Dream.

Her mother, Judy, believed in Hilary's talent and wanted to give her a chance to make a career of it. After her parents divorced, Hilary and her mother drove to Los Angeles in 1990 with $75 and one gas station credit card. They lived in their car for a few weeks until Judy found a job and somewhere to live.

Two years later, Hilary landed a role that showcased her immense talent. She played Brandon Teena, in *Boys Don't Cry* (1999). The film was based on the tragic true story of someone who is severely bullied and eventually murdered. This was a very difficult role to play. Hilary spent a long time studying people. Though she was only paid $3,000.00, Hilary knew that this opportunity to show that she could act was far greater in value than the money she received.

She received many awards for her performance.

She went on to play other roles in which she totally dedicated herself to studying the characters. She changed the way she ate and exercised for one role. She went Above and Beyond.

"I think everyone has a gift. You just have to be able to find it and follow your calling. People are afraid to do that. Some people are afraid of greatness, of success. And other people are afraid if they try and fail and that was their one big Dream, then what do they have left? I don't know what I did in this life to deserve all of this. I'm just a girl from a trailer park who had a Dream."

DECISIONS AND INITIATIVE
PART ONE OF THREE

"*Greatness is not a destiny granted to a few, but a decision available to anyone.***"**
Byron Reese, Author

Yes, Greatness is a choice that can be made by anyone. At any time. How amazing is that?

Decisions
"I make decisions one at a time, And no I never say I'm always right I'm confident that when I stand on my own, You'll see the truest form of a man when I'm shining through."
Avenged Sevenfold, Rock Band

Decision means making a commitment to do, be, or have something.

Henry Ford said, *"Those that think they can do, be, or have something and those that think they can't do, be or have something are usually right."*

It means those who think they can are right. And those who think they can't are right. We get what we think about. We are who/what we think.

How can you make **decisions** that will bring you closer to your Dream?

Whenever you have a major decision to make, ask yourself these four questions:

1. Do I truly want to be, do, or have this?
2. Will being, doing, or having this MOVE ME in the direction of my Dream?
3. Does being, doing, or having this agree with my values and morals?
4. Will being, doing, or having this hurt anyone?

If you answer YES to the first three and NO to the fourth, make the decision and get on with the creation of greatness.

Sometimes a decision may require extraordinary courage. Many of the greatest decisions we make, like those that affect our entire planet, are reached by taking great risks.

Think about the decision made by the fifty-six men who signed the Declaration of Independence in Philadelphia, July 4th, 1776. That Declaration claimed
Freedom—from Great Britain's influence—for everyone in the United States of America.

The decision was risky. The results of the decision could have meant a terrible end for many. But those involved did lots of critical thinking. Those involved asked questions, evaluated answers, and worked hard to make sure every angle was covered.

Can you think of two examples that involve life-changing decisions? You can choose something personal or from the history of someone else.

CHAPTER EIGHT | **DECISIONS AND INITIATIVE**

1)

_____

_____

2)

_____

_____

What impact did each of these decisions have on your life or the lives of others?

Example from a young student

A life-changing decision that affected me – by Jamie.

My grandparents moved to the United States when my mom was ten years old. They had lived in a country that was at war. My grandparents believed their daughter (my mom) would have a better life in the United States. They knew it would be difficult for them to learn a new language and understand another culture. They knew it might be difficult to find work. But they asked themselves lots of questions and they did some research and they made a life-changing decision.

They moved to the USA and learned to speak English, they worked hard at a business of sewing clothes, and they made a safe life for my mom.

This impacted me because I was born in the United States and know freedom. I can speak English and I can speak the first language of my grandparents. I can appreciate what hard work and good decision making can do to change a person's life—a whole family's life.

CHAPTER EIGHT | **DECISIONS AND INITIATIVE**

DECISIONS AND INITIATIVE
PART TWO OF THREE

Initiative

"Initiative is doing the right thing without being told." Victor Hugo, Playwright

Initiative means following up on an idea after a decision.

Initiative is like turning a key that opens a door to opportunity.

Once Jamie's grandparents decided to move to another country, they had to take the initiative to make sure they could get to that country. They didn't make the decision and then wait for a stranger to know they wanted to move. They found out what they had to do to move to the United States. And as soon as they knew what they had to do, they acted upon that information by, filling out forms, taking English lessons, applying for work, selling their possessions, buying a ticket to travel to the USA.

You probably show initiative all the time without even knowing that's what you're doing. Here are some ways:

You do things without being told.
You find out what you need to know.
You keep going when things get tough.
You recognize opportunities (that others might pass by).
You respond instead of reacting. (The small difference in words makes a big difference in action. Reacting is always a follow up without any thought. Responding is an action that is calmer and shows you have considered different options to the situation.

You've probably seen people take initiative in many ways. Here are some:

Someone practicing soccer skills before the coach shows up.
Someone reviewing notes before the teacher gets into the classroom.
Someone helping another student with some math.

When someone takes the initiative to do something, they show leadership skills and there's an energy associated with it. Initiative often brings about change and action.

Affirmation I am taking action after I make carefully considered decisions

DECISIONS AND INITIATIVE

PART THREE OF THREE

How to Develop Initiative

1. Make a Plan

"If you don't know where you are going, you'll end up someplace else."
Yogi Berra, Baseball Player

2. Build Self-Confidence

"No one can make you feel inferior without your consent."
Eleanor Roosevelt, First Lady

3. Spot Opportunities and Potential Improvements

"Opportunities never come a second time, nor do they wait for our leisure."
Booker T. Washington, Educator

4. Work Hard to research the answers that lead YOU to decision

"Genius is one percent inspiration, ninety-nine percent perspiration."
Thomas A. Edison, Inventor

5. Develop Persistence

"I may walk slowly but I never walk backward."
Abraham Lincoln, U.S. President

The ability to make good decisions and act on them is a highly valuable skill that will serve you well for the rest of your life.

Just like this book that needs to be read more than once, life skills need practice. It's no different to working out so you can be fit for an activity. And it takes time to build those muscles—the ones in your body (for a sport) and the ones in your brain (for greatness).

MY DREAM TRAINING COMMITMENT

I've chosen a Dream and now I AM transforming it to reality.

I will take an action each day that will bring me one step closer to my Dream.

I will do one thing each day without anyone telling me to do it.

I will take time to notice how the more I use my mind and body, the stronger my mind and body become.

I understand that developing good habits helps me make small changes—and those small changes (in my schoolwork or activities) will add up to big changes that bring me to my Dream.

I know that by taking initiative (following through after a decision) I will attract the attention of others who will recognize and support me in getting to my Dream.

_____

Signed/Date

*This agreement is based, in part, on the "Initiative and Leadership" statement in the book *Law of Success* by Napoleon Hill.

CHAPTER EIGHT | **DECISIONS AND INITIATIVE**

THINK SMARTER
PART ONE OF THREE

"Nothing is good or bad, except our thinking makes it so."
Ralph Waldo Trine, Author

Thinking Smarter is gathering the right information to allow you to make informed decisions toward the achievement of your Dream.

You must use your mind, not your emotions, to correctly understand, evaluate, and respond to events.

When you react emotionally, you are more likely to jump to conclusions and take things personally.

Example—someone trips you on the soccer field.
1) You immediately become angry (react, not respond).
2) You want to retaliate (how dare they trip you?).
3) You feel frustrated and remember other times you've been tripped.
4) You stay on the ground, angry, and are out of the play.

5) You retaliate and then serve a penalty yourself.

Slo-mo from the sidelines.
1) Someone trips on a wet spot on the grass.
2) He attempts to avoid you but accidentally slides into you.
3) You see you were not tripped on purpose.
4) You wish you would have just jumped up and continued to play because there was a perfect goal-scoring opportunity, which you missed because you were on the ground reacting.

Next time you are out on the field and you are "tripped":
1) Let it go—you don't have access to slo-mo.
2) Remember that an emotional outburst will take you out of the play.
3) Hop up immediately and continue to play.

What a difference between responding and reacting!

Can you think of a time when you reacted to an event emotionally, when instead you should have used accurate thinking?

_____

_____

_____

_____

Remember, YOU are in control of what you think.

THINK SMARTER

PART TWO OF THREE

When you are in control of your thinking, you are in control of your life!

Evaluating Information

You are constantly bombarded by information at any given time, and not all of it is important. Much of it will be opinion—even false.

It is vital that you be able to evaluate the credibility. Ask yourself:

1) What level of expertise does the source have?
Would a music teacher show you how to dribble a ball?

2) How up to date is your source?
If you were planning a weekend camping trip, you'd look at the weather forecast.

3) Who or what is influencing this source?

A newspaper article might actually be an advertisement. Or the writer of an article about sneakers might work for the company that makes them.

4) Am I examining this information with an open mind?
Be open to new ideas. That's the way to new possibilities.

"The test of an educated person: Can I entertain a new idea? Can I entertain another person? Can I entertain myself?"
Sidney Herbert Wood

Affirmation Today I CHOOSE high quality facts over information gathered quickly.

THINK SMARTER

PART THREE OF THREE

Intellectual Factors

You already know how to get information by sight, smell, touch, taste, and hearing, but you have intellectual factors as well—your mental muscles. They are perception, intuition, reasoning, memory, imagination, and "the will."

Intuition is like an inner computer that processes at a much higher speed than your other senses. It's sort of the "knowing before you know." It shows up as an "oh that doesn't feel right" or "I've got a hunch."

How can intuition show you the way to your Dream? When you have an idea that suddenly just pops into your head, don't immediately discredit it. This means your mental muscles were working behind the scenes. Ask yourself, "If I act on this idea, would it move me in the direction of my Dream?" If the answer is yes, you know what to do.

Perception

"People are always blaming their circumstances for what they are. I don't believe in circumstances. The people who get on in this world are the people who get up and look for the circumstances they want, and if they can't find them, make them."
George Bernard Shaw, Playwright

Perspective and Perception refer to every point of view and the feelings you have about those points of view.

When you perceive something, you "feel" it. Someone could say that the print in this book is grey and another could say it is black. Each has a different (viewpoint) and no one is wrong. You have perceived it to be black. The other person has perceived it to be grey. Each person has looked at the book with their own eyes and used their experiences in viewing other colors in order to decide what they think.

It's important to make an effort to view things from various angles, or perspectives—from every point of view. Effort to respect and understand the opinions of others is the key to becoming GREAT. Knowing there is more than one view of every situation opens up your world. Curiosity is a bonus. Creativity blows the doors off any thought patterns that held you in one spot.

You can change your perspective on anything, whether it's your current circumstances or the distance to your Dream. When we begin to open our minds to the way we view things, obstacles become opportunities.

Affirmation I AM happy and grateful to see the world with an open mind.

Reasoning means to apply extra thinking to your thinking.

The best way to train your Dream hasn't even been thought about. This entire book is based upon the idea that you have incredible power at your disposal to think, create, build, and execute big ideas. You have the power to decide how your Dream can best be achieved.

Choose something you already do. It can be simple or complex. Take a few minutes to open your mind and come up with a suggestion for yourself about a better way of doing it.

_____

_____

_____

Example:
Something I do is put my bike right by the front stoop so it's ready to ride first thing. I don't even go all the way down the steps, I just leap over and away I go. I love that. I don't even step on the sidewalk. Whoosh, I'm away.

Slight change:
It works well for me, but when it rains in the night, and I don't always know it's going to, I hop on and the seat is wet. Hey! Plastic bag. I'll keep one in the basket then cover the seat after I park the bike. No more wet butt.

Example:
Something I do every morning is grab an apple, a baggie of almonds, and a yogurt for lunch. It works for me — quick and healthy.

Slight change:
It makes more sense to take two yogurts or a piece of cheese with it because it's not enough food for lunch.

A little more reasoning: Why don't I line up five lunch bags in the fridge on Sunday night and put one apple and two yogurts and some cheese and almonds in each one. I could check if we have anything else to make each one different. That makes more sense, and think of the time I'll save. Oh, I just thought more about it—I get hungry in the afternoon—that's probably why I go to the vending machine during break. Taking a larger lunch will save me money.

A little more: Now my mind is on fire. Why don't I take a couple of extra minutes and make my brother's as well. Maybe he'd be willing to trade off then I'd only have to do lunches once every other week.

"Until thought is linked with purpose, there is no intelligent accomplishment."

James Allen, Philosopher

GET FIRED UP
PART ONE OF THREE

"Success consists of going from failure to failure without loss of enthusiasm.*" **Winston Churchill, Former British Prime Minister**

Enthusiasm means gusto, passion and zest. It is the spirit that transforms words and actions into contagious inspiration.

Contagious means "catchy" like a cold or flu can be catchy—but in this example in a "good" way.

When we listen to someone speak with enthusiasm, our moods lift. Things that seemed impossible are suddenly totally doable.

People who love what they do are said to be enthusiastic about their work. Some would describe this as "Being Fired Up."

Think of your Dream as a furnace and all the enjoyment you get out of imagining reaching your Dream is like throwing fuel into that furnace. You're building the fire and it's getting hotter and hotter.

"I just work hard and, as I always have done, believe I can do it. Most of all, though, I try to have fun."
Richard Branson, Business Magnate

Affirmation Today I AM charging up my mind and my body with enthusiasm.

Take a look at anyone who does something they love and you will see enthusiasm.

What types of activities are you enthusiastic about? Are you enthusiastic about school, sports, dance, church, music, reading, martial arts, Youth Scouting? What gets you excited?

_____

_____

_____

_____

GET FIRED UP
PART TWO OF THREE

The **Law of Vibration** states that everything is moving and everything is energy.

This subject "The Law of Vibration" may be unfamiliar to you. It is a part of the framework of a science called "quantum physics." Quantum Physics deals with phenomena (another word for wonders) on a microscopic scale.

This kind of science can be best explained with a "for instance." Look at your hand. It appears to be solid, but if you were to put it under an electron microscope, you would see tiny particles moving and being emitted.

Luckily, you don't need to be a quantum physicist to understand the Law of Vibration. It's easy to understand with an example. When you wake up, sometimes you feel good, and sometimes you don't. These feelings are vibrations. The best part of the Law of Vibration is that **YOU can change vibration by how you think and react.**

The first step to taking care of your enthusiasm and attitude is to pay attention to how you feel (to your vibration).

When you say to yourself, "I feel great today," what you are really saying is that you are in a positive vibration. When you lock into the "good" in your life, you stay in a positive vibration. Are you going to feel good all the time? No, of course not. This is when you need to push yourself to think of positive things to get past the negative and return to a state of good vibration.

Make a list of the good things in your life.
Then write how you can make each thing more amazing.

_____

_____

_____

_____

When you find ways to be more enthusiastic, you'll find the difficult situations begin to melt away as if by force of magic.

How to Maintain Enthusiasm after a Temporary Defeat

Michael Jordan was the athlete who was cut from the varsity basketball team in his sophomore year of high school. Angry and embarrassed, he began to get up early each morning to practice with the junior varsity coach. Eventually he made the varsity team again and became one of the most popular athletes in the world. Michael Jordan said, "I have missed more than nine thousand shots in my career. I have lost almost three hundred games. On twenty-six occasions, I was entrusted to take the game winning shot, and I missed. I have failed over and over and over again in my life. And that is why I succeed."

Affirmation I choose the positives and am enthusiastic about making my Dreams come true.

"Do the thing, and you will get the energy to do the thing."
Ralph Waldo Emerson, Philosopher

Enthusiasm is expressed to others in three ways: what you say, what you do, and what you think.

List ways your positive vibrations show through:

1) What have you said or what do you say that builds a positive life?

_____

_____

2) What have you done or what do you do that demonstrates enthusiasm?

_____

_____

Example:
How I build a positive life, by Joel.
I say good morning to the bus driver every day. He always smiles when I say that. I really do mean it because I remember one day when a dog ran out in the street and he swerved, and we were all okay, and so was the dog. I thought that was pretty awesome driving. Now that I've started saying good morning, I've heard some other kids saying it too.

And

Positive stuff I've done – by Mike
There was a new guy at school. He seemed sad. I told him it would be okay. I said I got lost finding the cafeteria when I first started. I told him about the great activities after school. The next day I called him over to sit with me and my friends at lunch. I remembered how it felt when I first started. Anyway, a few weeks later, I went to hockey camp and I didn't know anyone. Then I saw the new student; his brother runs the hockey school I signed up for. He thanked me for welcoming his younger brother.

Enthusiasm – by Taylor.
I always do four extra laps after practice. I love the feeling of the wind against

my face when I skate around the arena. The powerful strokes remind me how I love the speed in the game of hockey. I use the time to think about the next practice and remember how lucky I am to be able to play.

Enthusiasm and how it can lead to other things – by Janis
I've thought about how it would be great if everyone who wanted to play music could have an instrument. My friends and I organized a Facebook thing so that people could drop off unused music equipment at our community center. It started really small with a "please share this" then it became so big we had to use a computer program to list all the items. A music shop heard about us and sent us a letter saying they'd repair or tune the equipment for free. I never knew this would be so big, but there are fifty kids in an after school band and we've fundraised to hire a music teacher. I know it's big, but I'm really good with Dreaming big. It makes me feel good. I love it so much when people hear music; they seem so happy. I set up a post that thanked everyone for donating and promised some concerts when we get a little bit better.

When your thoughts, words, and actions come together through excitement, you change the world.

GET FIRED UP
PART THREE OF THREE

Sally Ride was born on May 26, 1951. She grew up in Los Angeles. She worked hard to go to university where she worked even harder and obtained a doctorate. Then she rose above one thousand other applicants for a spot in NASA's astronaut program.

After rigorous training, Sally Ride joined the Challenger shuttle mission and became the first American woman in space – June 18, 1983.

Later on, Sally Ride became the director of the California Space Institute at the University of California, San Diego, as well as a professor of physics at the school in 1989. In 2001, she started her own company to create educational programs and products known as Sally Ride Science to help inspire girls and young women to pursue their interests in science and math.

Sally Ride showed enthusiasm toward her studies and her career. Her excitement about science was so contagious that the lives of other students were changed.

Action Beyond Challenge

In the next few days, show your best friend why your favorite extracurricular activity is your favorite. Teach him or her something with all your heart so that he or she is excited to support you in achieving your Dream. Did he or she catch your enthusiasm to either join you or use the energy you shared to do something he or she loves? Did it make you feel good? Write about it here.

_____

_____

_____

_____

_____

_____

_____

_____

_____

_____

_____

_____

_____

_____

"Take control of the monster inside of you, focus the rage. All the answers are right there in front of you, just turn the page."
Otherwise, Rock Band

UNLEASH YOUR IMAGINATION
PART ONE OF THREE

"*Imagination is the true magic carpet.***"**
Norman Vincent Peale, Clergyman

Imagination is the ability to create and recreate. Imagination is like a super-power that lets you invent things, picture what might be, and even generate the feelings of what situations might feel like.

"*Creativity is thinking up new things. Innovation is doing new things.***"**
Hugh MacLeod, Cartoonist

Your imagination is unlimited. The best thing anyone can do for their Dream or their goal is to imagine it. When you imagine it (see it in your head), the only thing left to do is go after it.

You can use your imagination to rearrange old ideas into new combinations. It will help you convert failures into successes.

"There is a thinking stuff from which all things are made and which, in its original state, permeates, penetrates, and fills the interspaces of the universe. A thought in this substance produces the thing that is imaged by the thought. Man can form things in his thought, and, by impressing his thought upon the formless substance, can cause the thing he thinks about to be created."
Wallace D. Wattles, Author

What kinds of "things" would you like to create?

_____

_____

_____

_____

_____

_____

_____

_____

_____

_____

_____

_____

_____

_____

_____

_____

_____

_____

_____

_____

UNLEASH YOUR IMAGINATION
PART TWO OF THREE

Commit to play.
That's right, playing with paints, making costumes, exploring the woods, acting out stories, pretending to be a roller-skating dinosaur, and every other crazy idea that includes make-believe is how we develop our imaginations. We do this easily when we are little kids. Then, as we grow up, we forget to do it. We have more chores, homework, practices, and other responsibilities. We think it's not "grown up" to play.

The sky is NOT the limit; there are no limits.

It's important your imagination is applied to YOUR DREAM, not something someone else has said you have to do. And it's equally important your imagination be allowed to run wild. When other activities are forced on us and we are told "this will be your Dream," imagination doesn't work the same—it creates ways to get out of those forced activities.

When you watch television or play video games, you are actually being fed someone else's stories and images, and you're robbing yourself of the opportunity to Dream up your own. A little entertainment is fine, but too much puts you under the control of what someone else created.

"The man who has no imagination has no wings."
Muhammad Ali, Athlete

Do you remember using your imagination during play when you were younger? What did you like to do? Do you still give yourself these opportunities?

_____

_____

_____

Example – from Wanda
When I was little, I used the shed in the back yard to make a kind of log cabin. I always pretended I was an explorer, the kind that stayed out in the wild and dug for dinosaur bones. I loved sleeping out there at night and imagining I was in some remote part of the world with a crew of scientists who were also looking for ancient bones.

Do I still give myself these opportunities? Yes, I am thirteen and just learned about Dream Training last week. So I've opened up the shed, hung posters of dinosaur skeletons, taken my science books out there, and rigged up a light. I'm going to use it as my place to study because I want to be an archeologist. Today I hung a mirror in there so that I can say my affirmations in front of it. I AM going to become an archeologist. I'm looking forward to sleeping out there this weekend and imagining I'm in the arctic or I'm in the Badlands of Alberta on a big dig. I already feel so much more excitement than my usual enthusiasm. Hey! Isn't it cool that my learning time feels like play time?

Use your imagination to create plans for the achievement of your Dreams.

1) You may have to go back and reshape your Dream Worksheet.
2) Promise yourself the time and opportunity to expand your interests and find your special talents. Tell yourself you'll look for people and places who will inspire you.

3) Challenge yourself to read about new topics so that you can expand your mind. You will find your passion if you open your mind.

What do you wish you had more time to learn about? How can you make time for yourself to do this?

_____

_____

_____

Challenge yourself to keep growing abilities. Take risks, and don't be afraid of failure. Remember that on the road to Greatness, there will be failures because those very failures actually show you other ways to do things. Always look for improvement.

Remember Thomas Edison? He failed over ten thousand times before he successfully came up with a working light bulb. Had he not failed those times, he'd have never developed his life-changing invention.

"Everyone needs something to aim for. You can call it a challenge, or you can call it a goal. It is what makes us human. It was those challenges that took us from being cavemen to reaching for the stars."
Richard Branson, Business Magnate

How can I create new ways of training and learning that will be of benefit to others and myself?

_____

_____

_____

_____

_____

_____

There's always more than one way to do something.

What might work best for one person might not be the best way for you. Consider different ways to learn something. Let yourself find unusual ways to understand a problem and find a solution.

"If everyone is thinking alike, then somebody isn't thinking."
George S. Patton, US Army General

Use different techniques to grow your creativity.

Keep a creativity journal with you, and brainstorm with other people to come up with new ideas. Use your paper or electronic journal to keep track of ideas.

Paper is a great thing for doodling on. Some doodles became great inventions and solutions.

Organizing your thoughts by listing them and asking "what if" questions for each is a great way to develop ideas.

Using pictures instead of words works well, or pictures and words together in what is called a "mind map." Write or draw the central idea/subject in the middle of a piece of paper, then work your way outward in branches from the center with all your ideas that lead from that central subject. (You can take notes at school this way. Many people remember more when they make pictures instead of with their words.

UNLEASH YOUR IMAGINATION
PART THREE OF THREE

Time for Action

Get a large blank piece of paper, and map out the journey to your Dream. Now pick three of the steps needed to attain your Dream. For each step, list as many ways possible to do that step.

Your paper might end up looking like a flow chart or a treasure map. No matter, get the ideas down in words and pictures or symbols. (See next page for one you might want to use for inspiration.)

PROFILE OF PERSONAL SUCCESS:

If you have never heard of Steve Jobs, then know that he was a true technology visionary. He created Apple. His perseverance and belief in himself is one of the qualities that made him great.

Life's problems created the opportunity for Steve to use his mind power to focus on the things he wanted and not on the things he didn't want.

He said, *"Here's to the crazy ones. The misfits. The rebels. The troublemakers. The round pegs in the square holes. The ones who see things differently. They're not fond of rules. And they have no respect for the status quo. You can praise them, disagree with them, quote them, disbelieve them, glorify or vilify them. About the only thing you can't do is ignore them. Because they change things. They invent. They imagine. They heal. They explore. They create. They inspire.*

They push the human race forward. Maybe they have to be crazy. How else can you stare at an empty canvas and see a work of art? Or sit in silence and hear a song that's never been written? Or gaze at a red planet and see a laboratory on wheels? While some see them as the crazy ones, we see genius. Because the people who are crazy enough to think they can change the world, are the ones who do."

This statement is one of the most important ones made by a recent inventor-creator. Read it many time. Picture yourself as one of those people.

1. Write or draw your DREAM in the center starburst.
2. Write or draw related ideas in the other shapes (include names of people, places)
3. Add your affirmation or any other positive phrases around the outside.

WINNING PERSONALITY

PART ONE OF THREE

"Personality is only ripe when a man has made the truth his own."
Soren Kierkegaard, Philosopher

A personality is your own combination of your qualities and behaviors that make up your distinctive character.

Winning means being victorious, but it also means charming, captivating, cool, fun, and successful.

A winning personality refers to a person who uplifts others, is fun to be around, and is kind.

Which person would you hang with?

A complaining, know-it-all who puts you down and disses your ideas.

OR

A person who is enthusiastic about life, is genuine with you (that means honest/compliments your ideas and challenges you with questions), and is respectful in every way. Oh and makes you laugh until you pee your pants.

Of course you would choose the second person, so pack some extra underwear.

Having a pleasing personality will get you to your Dreams faster and in a more enjoyable way because other people will want to work with you and see you succeed. And they will succeed because you succeed. People with winning personalities end up including their friends in their projects or their friends indirectly benefit from the projects. In short, everybody wins.

Personality is not like height. You have total control over your personality, so you can improve any parts that might be a bit dull.

"Say what you mean but Always Love."
Islander, Rock Band

WINNING PERSONALITY
PART TWO OF THREE

How can you develop a winning personality?

Positive Mental Attitude
The achievement of your Dreams might rest solely on having a Positive Attitude. No one wants to be around a whiner or grouch. Smile, laugh, and focus on the good in your life. Be supportive and happy for others when they succeed.

Have Fun
Achieving your Dreams is about enjoying life. People like Drew Brees, Hope Solo, Lionel Andrés Messi, and LeBron James live and lived life to the fullest. People achieving their Dreams, like the musicians of Avenged Sevenfold and Otherwise, glow with pride. Successful people show a love of life and a passion for adventure.

Notice how successful people play at everything they do. They smile, they laugh—expressions of happiness pour out of them. The next time you see one of your heroes smile, you'll know why.

Be Respectful
Saying, "Please," "Thank you," and "Yes, ma'am/sir" are important qualities. Being nice says a lot about your attitude. When you are kind to someone, you are also being kind to yourself. You are showing the world you value yourself and others.

Good Sportsmanship & Teamwork
A pleasing personality will lead you to become a good teammate and develop sportsmanship. When you see greatness in others, you'll stand up and cheer, just like others will do so for you.

What is it about you that makes other people happy to be around you?

_____

_____

Is there anything you would like to improve on?

_____

_____

Think of three people you enjoy being around. What is it about each of their personalities that draws you to them?

_____

_____

_____

Affirmation Today I AM focused on the positive qualities of my personality.

WINNING PERSONALITY
PART THREE OF THREE

Lionel Andrés Messi is an Argentinian footballer who plays for La Liga club FC Barcelona. He is the team's all-time top scorer in all official club competitions. He captains the Argentinian national team.

In 2012, Messi made UEFA Champions League history by becoming the first player to score five goals in one match. He also became the first player to lead the league in scoring in four successive Champions League campaigns. He set the world record for most goals scored in a season during the 2011–12 season, with seventy-three goals. In the same season, he set the current goal scoring record in a single La Liga season, scoring fifty goals.

"It doesn't matter if he is playing in front of ten spectators or 100,000. Leo is the same as always, he always feels secure and has the same desire to win. He is the boy who says: 'Give me the ball, I want to play, I want to be creative, I want to show my talents.'"
Frank Rijkaard, Former Dutch International and Barcelona Coach

Messi spoke about the most difficult moments in his life: "Moving from Argentina to Spain when I was 13 years old. The first few years here were tough. There were times when my father and I were in Barcelona and the rest of the family was in Rosario. We were suffering. I missed Matias, Rodrigo, my little sister and my mother. I used to cry alone in my house so that my father wouldn't see.

"All kids want to be footballers, but in order to make it you have to go through some very tough times, like when I decided to stay in Barcelona…it was my decision. No one forced me to make it. My parents asked me many times what I wanted to do. I wanted to stay in the youth academy because I knew that was my chance to be a footballer. I was very responsible from a very young age."

Messi has said about overcoming his growth problems and using his height to his advantage:

"I was a child. I didn't really have any idea of what was happening to me, apart from the injections in my legs every night. But, being smaller, I have learned to control the ball better on the ground, be more agile and faster than the bigger players in order to keep the ball.

"I have fun like a child in the street. When the day comes that I'm not enjoying it, I will leave football. I'm lucky to be part of a team who help to make me look good, and they deserve as much of the credit for my success as I do for the hard work we have all put in on the training ground.

"I prefer to win titles with the team, ahead of individual awards or scoring more goals than anyone else. I'm more worried about being a good person than being the best football player in the world. When all this is over, what are you left with? When I retire, I hope I am remembered for being a decent guy."

CREATING OPEN SPACE

PART ONE OF THREE

"When you're clear about your purpose and your priorities, you can painlessly discard whatever does not support these, whether it's clutter in your cabinets or commitments on your calendar." Victoria Moran, Author

What is the Law of Open Space?
That nature will fill an open space with goodness.

If there is something you wish to have happen in your life, you must first create the space for it. If you are holding onto old clutter or negativity, there is no room for the positive to come into your life.

1) Create open space by ridding yourself of something you no longer want or need.

2) Visualize the space filled with exactly what you want in its place.
This will require some thought and work on your part—creative, fun work.

"Some people believe holding on and hanging in there are signs of great strength. However, there are times when it takes much more strength to know when to let go and then do it."
Ann Landers, Advice Columnist

Releasing the things that hold you down is a big process, but you can start with small steps until you have achieved the space needed to fulfill your Dreams.

How to Create the Space to make good things happen in YOUR life.

Get rid of things you don't use anymore—that includes broken things.

Want better grades? Start with cleaning out your desk or room to create a space that helps you study and keep better track of your assignments and notes.

Do you have a closet full of clothes or toys that you don't use? Get rid of them, and you will find that your closet refills again, with things that you'll use.

Do you wish you had more time to train your Dream? Create that time by removing the time-wasters. Maybe you'll have to stop watching four TV shows and watch only one. Or spend less time on the Internet.

What clutter can you remove from your room?

_____

_____

How will you remove that clutter? And when will you remove it?

_____

_____

What about in your backpack? Any there?

_____

_____

How will you remove that clutter? And when will you remove it?

_____

_____

What clutter can you remove from your mind?

_____

_____

How will you remove that clutter (those thoughts)? And when will you re-move them?

_____

_____

CREATING OPEN SPACE
PART TWO OF THREE

When you free up space for inspiring people you'll open yourself to healing, vibrant, and beneficial energy.

If you have "friends" in your life who say negative things, purposefully bring others down, or try to convince you to do things that you know are not right, it may be time to create some space.

Bob Proctor said it best, *"I mix with people that I KNOW are going to support me. That I KNOW want me to support them. That are goal-oriented, that are locked into what they want to do, and know that they can do it. I absolutely refuse to spend a lot of time with anyone else...Do I spend time with other people? Sure. Do I hear people complain? Yeah. I just don't want to relate to it any more. I've lived there. It's like Sophie Tucker said. 'I've been rich and I've been poor. Rich is better.'"*

Saying no to invitations from people is okay. Do you think you can do this? How might you go about it?

Creating space by letting others go is not a bad thing and doesn't mean you don't like those people. If there are negative people in your life, can you forgive them and then move on?

Are there people you can spend less time with?

Are there people you can spend more time with?

Your outer life is what your inner thoughts and feelings have made. It's like your thoughts and feelings are a factory and they create the product called your outer life.

When you release old patterns of negative thinking and replace them with powerful positive thoughts that make you feel hopeful and happy, you begin bringing in goodness. It's like you've started a new factory that manufactures amazing stuff.

One player on a girls' soccer team used to read this affirmation every time there was a break to switch training:

"I AM a strong, smart, confident, beautiful, and powerful person. I need these qualities to be the best human I can be. I believe in myself and will not allow anyone interfere with the achievement of my Dreams. Whatever my mind can imagine and believe, my mind can achieve."

It's true—only when you believe it can you achieve it.

What are some of the affirmations you've created since beginning this book? Do you have any new ones?

_____

_____

_____

_____

KNOWING WHEN TO LET GO

If something is not right in your life, you may be ignoring the messages that are being sent to you. The more you rely on your inner guidance, the more you will trust it when it warns you to shift direction.

Sometimes just a little shift is all that is needed to create open space for the goodness to flow in.

"Intuition is always right in at least two important ways. It is always in response to something. It always has your best interests at heart"
Gavin de Becker, Author, Security Specialist

What small shifts can you create to make some space to start moving toward your Dreams? (Trust that even a smile will make a difference.)

_____

_____

_____

How can you start this process today?

_____

_____

Remember, this is a never-ending process. You must continue creating space for the good you wish to receive.

CREATING OPEN SPACE
PART THREE OF THREE

PROFILE OF PERSONAL SUCCESS:

Richard Branson was born on July 18, 1950, in Surrey, England. His father, Edward James Branson, worked as a lawyer and his mother as a flight attendant. When Richard was younger, he had a learning challenge called dyslexia. Dyslexia involves having some confusion about the shape and order of letters and numbers. Richard came close to failing the school he attended before he was thirteen. After that he went to a boarding school. A boarding school is where students attend school and live there.

At age sixteen, Richard dropped out of school and started a magazine called *Student*. He sold advertising in the magazine (that means he charged money for businesses to announce their services and products). The first fifty thousand copies were given out for free because the advertising had covered the cost of producing the magazine. By 1969 he lived with a group of musicians. It was then he decided to start a mail-order record company called Virgin. He thought it would help fund his magazine efforts.

The company did okay, and Richard made enough money to open a record shop in London. The shop was successful and Richard built a recording studio and started Virgin Records. His record company became one of the top ones in the world.

Richard was able to invest in other businesses, and the Virgin Group moved into many countries and became involved in trains, phones, and even space tourism. He also followed other Dreams and became involved in sporting events and in an epic balloon adventure.

Although he became a billionaire, he continued to be an adventurer and set more goals. He involved himself in helping others and he received many awards.

His own words speak about success and failure, and about the joy of adventure.

"Throughout my life I have achieved many remarkable things. Today we are increasingly aware of the effects of our actions on the environment, and I strongly believe that we each have a responsibility, as individuals and organizations, to do no harm.

"I set goals and then work out how to achieve them. Anything I want to do in life I want to do well, and not half-heartedly.

"My first money-making scheme was when I was about nine years old. One Easter I came up with a great plan. I would grow Christmas trees. The bag of seeds cost just $5 and we would sell each tree for $2. Sadly, rabbits ate all the seedlings but we did make a small profit on the rabbit pie.

"It's easy to give up when things are hard but I believe we have to keep chasing our Dreams and our goals. And once we decide to do something, we should never look back, never regret it."

LEADERSHIP AND TEAMWORK
PART ONE OF THREE

"If you want to lift yourself up, lift up someone else."
Booker T. Washington, Educator

Leadership
Great leaders and great team players share many of the same qualities. Great leaders are the best team players because they are able to bring out the best qualities of each person around them.

When you have strong purpose and support the goals of your team, you will earn the respect of your teammates.

Affirmation Whatever I do, to or for another person, I do, to myself. It's the law of nature.

"I'll never forget that I am just one person. Without the help of my teammates, I couldn't do anything."
Lionel Messi, Athlete

Cooperation is the beginning of all organized effort. Cooperation is how we are able to survive. Your family is the very first team you ever joined.

When you were born, you weren't able to feed or clothe yourself, so your family worked together to keep you healthy, warm, and safe. As you've grown, you've become an active member in your family's team. Maybe you contribute by helping with gardening or laundry.

"My brothers were found on the basketball court. It was about playing well and winning big; but most of all it was a story about five boys from varying backgrounds who came together as best friends."
LeBron James, Basketball Player

Beyond your family, you are a team player in your community. This can include your school, your neighborhood, your church, and other groups or teams you join.

What are some of the teams you are a part of right now? (Don't forget to consider part of your family, community, school, helping roles, and sports.)

You owe it to each of your teams to be the best teammate you can possibly be. *It's all the little things added together that lead to victory. The road to a Super Bowl win is a process of bringing a team together and accomplishing your goals, step by step. We were teammates, bound by the blood, sweat, and tears of many years of struggle, and we were ready to fight. We'd go onto the field, stick together no matter what, and do all we could to defeat a worthy opponent. Ha-ooh!"*
Drew Brees, NFL Saints Quarterback

How can you be a good teammate at home? At school? During gym? What other examples can you think of?

LEADERSHIP AND TEAMWORK
PART TWO OF THREE

How to be a Great Team Player (and Leader)

Honesty

When you chose to be honest in the games and sports you play, and also in your life, you inspire everyone around you to do the same. You raise the standards of the game, the team, and the community.

Communication

Clear communication is important to accomplish goals. Remember that listening is often more important than speaking. When you are listening, you are learning about something or someone. When you are speaking, you are talking about something you already know. Listening is more valuable than most realize. Ask questions when you don't understand. Listen and then really think about the answers.

Positive Attitude

Occasionally things won't work right or mistakes will be made. When this happens, keep a positive attitude and work together to fix it. Getting upset and playing the blame game never fixes anything.

Confidence
When you have confidence in yourself, your coaches, and your teammates, you trust their skills as well as yours.

Commitment
When everyone sticks to their commitment, incredible things begin to happen. Don't give up, and if you see that a teammate is struggling, encourage him.

Creativity
Use your creativity to solve challenges and come up with better ways to train and improve.

Be a good sport
Nobody wins all the time. Play your best, play fair, and be gracious to everyone, whether they are on your team or not. Don't lose your cool over little things.

"The edge is knowing that you are getting to your goals and treating people right along the way because, as good as you can be, you are so focused that you need regular people around you to balance and help you."
Mark Cuban, Business Magnate

"Our ongoing goal was to break the team record for the number of times heading the ball. Usually we could get around seventy headers back and forth without letting the ball touch the ground. That day, heading to each other across a little path that led into the woods, while my father watched, we broke our record, keeping the ball up for eighty-eight touches."
Hope Solo, Soccer Player

"While other bands see making music as a job, we want to make great music the kids love."
Avenged Sevenfold, Rock Band

LEADERSHIP AND TEAMWORK

PART THREE OF THREE

The Man Who Thinks He Can

If you think you are beaten, you are
If you think you dare not, you don't,
If you like to win, but you think you can't
It is almost certain you won't.
If you think you'll lose, you've lost
For out of the world we find,
Success begins with a fellow's will
It's all in the state of mind.
If you think you are outclassed, you are
You've got to think high to rise,
You've got to be sure of yourself before
You can ever win a prize.
Life's battles don't always go
To the stronger or faster man,
But soon or late the man who wins

Is the man WHO THINKS HE CAN!
Walter D. Wintle

Write about a time when you made your team, group, and/or class better.

_____

_____

If this is difficult, write about what you could do to make your team, group, and/or class better.

_____

_____

PROFILE OF SUCCESS:

Avenged Sevenfold (A7X) is an American rock band from Huntington Beach, California. Its members are vocalist M. Shadows, lead guitarist Synyster Gates, rhythm guitarist Zacky Vengeance, bassist Johnny Christ and drummer Arin Illjay.

A7X on their Dream of making music: *"We originally just wanted to be a band that played the music we wanted and sound different than anyone else. That's happened, but along with that people are saying that we have been leading the comeback of metal. I don't know if that's good or bad. If other kids want to start metal or rock bands because of us then that's great, but we will just continue to do our thing."*

Avenged Sevenfold came onto the music scene with a metalcore sound. Their first album contained screaming vocals and heavy guitar riffs. The band changed their style later and more of a mainstream hard rock. They explored new sounds and created lots of interesting music. Then their drummer, James Sullivan, "The Rev," died of an apparent drug overdose in 2009. This was a strong lesson to them, and to all, that drugs and alcohol can kill off your ambitions and Dreams before your 'greatness' is realized.

The band continued with drummer Mike Portnoy and released their fifth album, Nightmare, in 2010.

A7X on the power of believing in yourself, your music and your fans:

"If anything happens we don't ever fall, it's like they're holding us up. We're not on the radio, but everywhere we go we always have this rabid group of fans. We would've never had that if we had some lucky break and just jumped to the point we're at now. I hope it gradually keeps going up. The slower you go the more it keeps building underneath you and we're grateful for that."

Avenged Sevenfold has released five studio albums, one live album/compilation, and fifteen singles. They are leaders in the New Wave of American Heavy Metal and received second place on Ultimate Guitar's Top Ten Bands of the Decade.

Who is your favorite musician or band? Why?

_____

_____

_____

How did your favorite musician/musicians get to where they are today?

_____

_____

_____

Action Beyond Paper

Not only do you need to be a good teammate to get on in this world, but many young children are in need of someone to set a standard of leadership. Who is someone you know that you could mentor and share your Dream with?

_____

_____

Using your Dream plan, show someone or a group of people something that you're doing to achieve your Dream.

For example, a boy named Timothy stood in front of his fourth grade class and taught them how to juggle a soccer ball with their feet.

When you share your Dream, you will get closer to it and you will inspire others.

BLESSINGS IN DISGUISE
PART ONE OF THREE

"Out of struggle and use comes strength."
Ralph Waldo Emerson, Philosopher

A **Blessing in Disguise** is an old phrase that means "something bad came along but it actually turned out to be good."

It's like when a sudden rainstorm soaks you, but waters the dry garden at your home. It's any difficult, challenging, or seemingly impossible situation that you survive then see there was a bonus to having gone through that difficult time.

The important thing in moving toward your Dream is to decide how you're going to handle the curveballs.

Always Persist
If you can survive your challenges and keep on trying, you will reach your Dreams. Defeat is a destructive force only when it is accepted as

failure. You have not failed unless you accept temporary defeat as failure.

Too often people give up without realizing how close they have come to the golden moment.

When you've gone as far as you can, allow yourself to rest. Then keep going.

"Courage doesn't always roar, sometimes it's the quiet voice at the end of the day whispering, 'I will try again tomorrow.'"
Mary Anne Radmacher, Author

Affirmation The difficult times are stepping stones to my Dreams.

Become Better, Not Bitter.
Don't let yesterday or last year define tomorrow or next year.

Adversity (hardship, difficulty) is overcome by moving forward. Nothing you can do, say, think, or feel will ever change the past. Accept what has happened, and let go of everything that does not serve you or make you feel healthy and well. Anger, shame, guilt, bitterness, and all other negative emotions are poison.

"The truth is, unless you let go, unless you forgive yourself, unless you forgive the situation, unless you realize that the situation is over, you cannot move forward."
Steve Maraboli, Author

You have control over your reaction to adversity. After you go through a loss, it is normal to be sad, but that sadness should not become a way of life. Without experiencing occasional pain and sorrow, you would be unable to appreciate pleasure and joy. Keep a positive mental outlook, and remember—everything in life is temporary.

Adversity (difficulty, pain, suffering, frustration, sadness) is like a hurricane, destroying everything before it. Everything, that is, except the indestructible.

When we experience difficulties, we are able to see the truth about ourselves. We often get really clear about what we want in life.

Overcoming adversity is essential for a healthy, thriving life. It builds mental strength, character, compassion, and endurance.

"You may encounter many defeats, but you must not be defeated. In fact, it may be necessary to encounter the defeats, so you can know who you are, what you can rise from, how you can still come out of it."
Maya Angelou, Author

Life's lessons will be repeated until learned.

Very often, you may notice that difficult times come over and over. When you notice this happening, you need to listen. Those messages (bad things) will keep happening until you are able to learn what life is saying to you.

Your own awareness and your ability to change are necessary to understand this important rule of life—lessons are repeated until learned.

"Life first will send the lesson to you in the size of a pebble; if you ignore the pebble, then life will send you a brick; if you ignore the brick, life will send you a brick wall; if you ignore the brick wall, life will send you a demolition truck."
Oprah Winfrey, Talk show host, Business Magnate

Helping
Be part of the solution and encourage yourself as well as others. The difference in you being happy or miserable comes from the words within your heart, so offer kind, positive, life-changing words to those in need, including yourself.

Sometimes the very words we say to a friend are the words we need to say to ourselves.

BLESSINGS IN DISGUISE
PART TWO OF THREE

An Attitude of Gratitude

It is important to be grateful for things in life when times are good and when they are difficult, especially when they are difficult.

When we focus on positives and being grateful, we shift toward seeing more goodness. We bring about what we think about. This is the basis for the Law of Attraction and Vibration.

"There's nothing here to take for granted with each breath that we take, The hands of time strip youth from our bodies. And we fade, memories remain as time goes on."
Avenged Sevenfold, Rock Band

Example—everyone likes to feel appreciated, right? If you are making an effort to please someone and they are consistently rude and ungrateful, you're going to stop hanging around them. However, if they are always happy and grateful to see you, it makes you feel good inside, and you will want to spend more time with them.

The good things in your life have come to you through the natural laws of the Universe. Gratitude keeps you bouncing along in happiness and prevents you from falling into negative patterns.

As you show more gratitude, more things will come to you that you can be grateful for.

Without gratitude, you may find yourself experiencing (and expecting) constant disappointment. This is a dangerously rocky road.

Remember autosuggestion? That is when a message is repeated over and over and we begin to believe it. A reminder—it works the same for all messages, positive or negative.

Think about some people you know. Some say, "The better it gets the better it gets." They seem to always be in a state of happiness.

Then some say, "The worse it gets the worse it gets" or "when it rains it pours." For those people, they always seem to be in a state of unhappiness.

Affirmation "I am so happy and grateful for …"

BLESSINGS IN DISGUISE
PART THREE OF THREE

GRATITUDE LIST WORKSHEET

Grab a blank sheet of paper. List ALL the things you are grateful for.

Write your name and the date on your list. Keep it in a safe place so that you can find it next month.

Every month, repeat this exercise. Notice (over time) if you have even more things to be grateful for.

PROFILE OF SUCCESS:

Oprah Winfrey was born in a small farming community in the town of Kosciusko, Mississippi, on January 29, 1954. Her growing up years were unstable and she suffered abuse from some of the grownups around her.

Eventually, she moved to Nashville to live with her father, Vernon, a barber and businessman. She attended Tennessee State University in 1971 and then began working in radio and television broadcasting in Nashville.

Her warm-hearted personal style impressed people all over the world. Over the years, she grew a business empire and became—according to Forbes magazine—the wealthiest African American of the twentieth century. She is said to be one of the most influential women of her generation. Oprah is known for always expressing her gratitude and for helping others. She worked hard to become a leader in the business world and she never lost her sense of gratitude or her belief in caring for others. She is often quoted because what she says is filled with goodness and common sense. She achieved greatness through hard work and gratitude.

"Books were my pass to personal freedom. I learned to read at age three, and soon discovered there was a whole world to conquer that went beyond our farm in Mississippi."
Oprah Winfrey

MY BODY TEMPLE

PART ONE OF THREE

" *Take care of your body; it's the only place you have to live.*"
Jim Rohn, Entrepreneur

Yes, your body is like a house you live in. It's important to have your great mind in a healthy body.

It needs a lot of care. Inactivity makes a body weak, and in turn makes it easy for negative feelings and behaviors to take hold. Our bodies were meant to move. When we move, our brains become stronger.

Being physically fit includes benefits to your mental state (the way you think when you write and do math), emotional health (the way you feel and respond), and spiritual being (the way in which you are settled and comfortable with your place in the universe).

Access to fresh air, nutritious food, wholesome and creative thinking, and physical activity are all totally under your control.

Walk the dog, walk someone else's dog, ride your bike, take the stairs, play games, run around, fly a kite. Enjoy the freedom of having mobility.

Before moving on to the exercise and nutrition specifics, write down the activities you enjoy.

_____

_____

_____

_____

_____

And the activities you'd like to try.

_____

_____

_____

_____

_____

MY BODY TEMPLE

PART TWO OF THREE

Moving around in fun activities and adding movement to your day, like taking the stairs or walking the dog, are great habits to get into. To kick it up a notch, strength training is important as is nutrition.

Strength training and cardiovascular (heart) fitness is important. Below is a basic workout routine based on the workouts of the Marine Corps.

This is a workout you can control and modify to suit your fitness level over time. Be a "beast" and challenge yourself. How great is that? You're going to work out like a Marine.

The core of the Marine's fitness program is called the Daily Seven. It is a series of exercises that are done before a run and/or a strength training session.

It is suggested that the Daily Seven become part of your routine at least three days a week. Allow one day between workouts to allow your muscles to recover.

Daily Seven
Do one set of each of the following exercises: jumping jacks, cherry pickers, bend and thrust, mountain climbers, trunk twists, Marine push-ups, and lunges.

Do what you can and then increase (don't reduce) adding additional sets as you become more fit.

The Exercises

Jumping Jacks: stand with your arms at your sides. Hop up and spread your legs just wider than your shoulders. At the same time, swing your arms up and touch them above your head. Return to the starting position.

Cherry Pickers: stand with your arms at your sides. Lean over and touch the ground in front of you as far out as you can without losing your balance, then touch the ground between your legs and finally the ground behind your legs before returning to the starting position.

Bend and Thrust: stand with your arms at your sides. Squat down and put your hands on the ground. Thrust your legs out behind you to assume the push-up position. Reverse until you are standing again.

Mountain Climbers: begin by squatting down with your hands on the ground. One leg should be extended and one tucked up under you. Begin switching the position of the legs back and forth.

Trunk Twists: stand with your arms on your hips and lean forward, to the left side, back and to the right side in a broad circular motion.

Marine Push-Ups: lay face down on the ground with your feet together and balancing on your toes. Have your hands on the ground at shoulder width apart with the arms tucked at the sides. Push off the ground until just before your elbows lock. Keep your back straight. Lower yourself back to the ground, only touching your chest to the ground.

Lunges: from a standing position with your hands on your hips, step forward with one foot and lower the opposite knee to the ground. Push back with your extended foot until you are standing again. Switch legs.

For an added strength workout, do three sets of ten repetitions of each of the following: pull-ups, push-ups, squats, lunges and diamond push-ups. (A diamond push-up is where the hands are placed under the chest and the thumbs and index fingers form a diamond. The shift in the hand positioning changes which muscles are worked in the exercise.)

Cardiovascular Training
A healthy heart and circulatory system improves our quality of life. We live longer when we have a healthier cardiovascular system. This activity should be something you enjoy.

Play outside
Walk fast for time or distance
Jog for time or distance
Jump rope for time or repetitions
Sprint on flat ground
Sprint up a gentle hill
Spring down a gentle decline
Walk and/or run stairs
Hike
Bike
Swim
Enjoy racquetball, tennis, basketball, either recreationally or organized

"The first wealth is health."
Ralph Waldo Emerson, Philosopher

Profile of Success

Hope Amelia Solo is an American soccer goalkeeper, and considered one of the best goalkeepers in the world. After playing soccer for University of Washington, she played for multiple international leagues and soccer clubs. She also played goalie for the U.S. Women's Olympic Team. Through focus and dedication, Hope Solo trained herself into an incredible athlete, once even goalkeeping for 1,054 minutes without giving up a single goal.

"I'm a firm believer in bodyweight exercises and plyos. I lift weights, but minimally. I do a ton of push-ups and sit-ups, both with stability balls. I also do pull-ups, lunge jumps, squat jumps, box jumps and jump rope work, which, surprisingly, really works my arms.

"It's definitely hard to maintain our diets when we're on the road so much, and
especially in different countries. I find it even more difficult here in China. Fortunately we travel with a blender and still get to make our soy protein shakes. I take supplements throughout the year, but leading into a major event, I stick to multivitamins to get me through the tournament." *

*note: if you are using soy products, make sure that they are organic and non-genetically modified, or use almond milk.

"When I am with the Olympic team we do a ton of on the field, position-specific work. That means lots of diving, and getting up and diving again for me. It's exhausting. However when we have time off, I focus more on plyometrics, footwork, speed, agility, and endurance. I'm able to work on specific footwork that actually allows me to dive.

"In the off-season training, I enjoy yoga. Prior to training and games, I don't stretch in excess. We like to call it dynamic stretching. I like to keep my muscles tight and springy for quickness.

"Athletes are extremists. When they're training, it's laser focus."

When you do the Marine Corps Daily Seven, write down how many of each exercise you can do. Keep track and see how you improve over time.

MY BODY TEMPLE

PART THREE OF THREE

Nutrition
We are what we eat. Good food is necessary for our brains and bodies to work well.

Begin with drinking enough water. Our bodies are about 70% water. Drink lots every day because we sweat it out and pee it out, so it's important that we stay hydrated. Avoid sports drinks, which are loaded with sugar. Coconut water is a good choice in place of commercial sports drinks because it is naturally packed with electrolytes and other nutrients.

All foods should be eaten in moderation. Eat a balanced diet that includes getting lots of leafy veggies and some fibrous ones. Fruits are important too. Any natural nutrition article can point you in the right direction, but if you think of eating things that are in their natural state (the way nature made them and not the way man altered them), that is an excellent start.

Know that there are healthy fats. Our body needs fats to insulate and protect us. Healthy fats include nut butters, coconut oil, and olive oil. Eggs, beans and fish are among food that contain fat and protein.

Remember, natural is the way to go. Think about whether nature made the food; if nature didn't, don't eat it. A drinkbox filled with orange colored liquid isn't even close to the orange from a tree. Apple fruit gummies are not apples. Natural tasting fruit rollups are not fruit. Compare everything to what it is supposed to resemble, and then consider how far away from its original source it is.

Whole grains are whole-wheat flour, cracked wheat, oatmeal, whole cornmeal, brown rice, and quinoa. Breads and pastas made from these are healthier than those made from only white flour. Think about white flour being like glue. If your body is 70% water and you put white flour (bread, bagels, cakes, donuts) into your body what will that make? You've probably made stuff out of paper mache at school. Flour and water makes glue.

If you keep the foods you know are junk food low, you will notice a difference and you will not feel deprived. Avoid or keep these foods low, and never have artificial sweeteners like aspartame or other chemicals found in soda. It is best to avoid soda anyway because of the high artificial sugar content.

Stay away from: cakes, candy, cookies, pastries, and donuts. Sodas, energy drinks, sports drinks, and fruit "flavored" drinks. Pizza made with white flour and solid fats. Ice cream. Sausages, hot dogs, bacon and other processed meats that contain nitrates.

Avoid margarine, shortening or anything fried in trans fats (which are man-made chemicals).

The fewer ingredients on the label, and the closer the item is to nature, 16. · Don't be fooled by pictures on wrappers. If it's in a box or a al.

How many different vegetables and fruits can you think of that match each color?

Yellow- _____

White- _____

Orange- _____

Blue- _____

Purple- _____

Red- _____

Pink- _____

Green- _____

Brown- _____

Black- _____

Can you think of other colored vegetables/fruits?

_____

_____

Challenge: See how many different colored vegetables/fruits you can eat each day.

Tips to getting the right foods in your body:

Make half your plate veggies and fruits.
Eat your colors.

Eat whole grains and plenty of fiber.

Stay away from sugar.

Read the ingredients on labels, not just the nutritional facts.

Drink as much water as you can.

Eat a balanced amount of food in as natural form as possible.

Affirmation Today I will focus on creating healthy habits that will benefit my entire body and mind.

TIME AND MONEY SMARTS
PART ONE OF THREE

We each have the same twenty-four hours in a day. Most students have eight hours of school, eight hours of sleep, and eight hours of "free" time.

Realizing it is "free" time is amazing because once you've made up your mind to work toward a Dream, you can use the "free" time to make it happen.

Free time can be packaged in ways that make the days feel endless—in a good way.

Six questions to ask yourself about how you currently spend your time

1) I spend too much of my time on:

_____

_____

2) I don't have enough time for:

_____

_____

3) I spend: (circle one) too much/not enough/just enough time on home-work.
I could better manage my homework time by:

_____

_____

4) I spend: (circle one) too much/not enough/just enough time on activi-ties and sports.
I could better manage my activity time by:

_____

_____

5) One sport, club or activity I wouldn't want to drop is

_____

because _____

_____

6) My favorite way to spend my free time is:

_____

_____

Block out the eight hours of free time on a piece of paper. You might want to make it sixteen half-hour blocks or thirty-two fifteen-minute blocks. Make sure to plan time to relax. See if you can combine working toward your Dream (practices or workouts) with fun, because your Dream needs to be something you want and love to do.

TIME AND MONEY SMARTS
PART TWO OF THREE

"*I strongly believe that the earlier you can start teaching kids how to manage their money, the better equipped they'll be when they get to college, start a business, or into their careers.*"
Drew Brees, NFL Saints Quarterback

The following sections are based on information from PBSKids.org. Check out all their online information and exercises at http://pbskids.org/itsmylife/money/managing/index.html

Spending and Saving Money

If you have some money, that's great. Maybe you deliver papers or babysit. You might receive a check for your birthday or allowance from your parents. Money that comes to us from all sources is called income.

Having an income is a good thing. It's also a responsibility. You have to make choices about what to do with it. Remembering you worked a lot of hours for the money to buy one pizza and a soda might make you think twice about buying that take-out. If you are saving for a new bike, making a sandwich and not buying pizza will get you the bike faster. Managing money is about balance.

What do you currently spend your money on?

_____

_____

How do you decide when to spend and when to save?

_____

_____

Can you do a little bit of both? A little spending and a little saving? That's the best way. If you learn the ways to save and spend responsibly, then you'll never feel deprived, and you'll be happy and secure in the now and in the future.

Needs versus Wants

Saving means setting aside a certain amount of money each time you get paid.
Say you get $5.00 a week and save $3.00 of it (each week). After a month you'll have $12.00, after two months $24.00, and six months $72.00.

Sometimes you have to spend money, like on bus fare or for a new tire for your bike. Other times you might spend money on something you want, like a music download or videogame.

In order to know when to spend and when to save, it helps to know the difference between needs and wants.

"I have to have that pair of jeans" or "I need to see that movie." Sound familiar?

Will something horrible happen if those jeans are not purchased or the movie is not viewed? Often times a few pairs of jeans in the back of the closet have never been worn. As for the blockbuster, it'll be on TV in a month. These are wants.

Needs are things that you can't be without. Nutritious food, a place to live, a warm winter coat, a good pair of shoes, bus fare.

And there are times when wants become needs. If a person lives far from school, it's too far to walk, and there is no bus route, a bike becomes a need.

Questions to ask when figuring out your own needs and wants:

• What items do I need in order to get ready in the morning? A toothbrush, towel, shampoo?
• How about clothes? Shoes, socks, pants, and a sweater?
• How do I get to school? Bus fare, bike, skateboard, decent walking shoes?
• Are there things I need for school? Books, backpack, pens, calculator?
• Do I have to supply sports equipment for my activities?

Other examples that show need versus want.

• NEED a toothbrush for hygiene. WANT a blue toothbrush instead of a green one because you prefer blue. Both will clean your teeth.
• NEED a sweater to keep you warm. WANT a designer version of a sweater that costs $50.00 more than another brand. Both will keep you warm.
• NEED a bike to get to school. WANT a twenty-one-speed mountain bike with metallic paint. Both will provide transportation.
• NEED a backpack to carry your school stuff. WANT a knapsack with a designer logo. Both will hold your books.

Write a list of things you believe necessary for your day-to-day existence. Why do you feel these things are necessary?

_____

_____

_____

_____

Make a list of things that you want? Why do you want these things?

_____

_____

_____

_____

Are any of your wants also needs?

Now that you have an idea of the things you need versus the things you want, it's important to set money goals so you can actually save and spend wisely.

TIME AND MONEY SMARTS
PART THREE OF THREE

Set Money Goals

It's easier to save money when you have set some goals than when you don't have a plan. Successful people think about what they want to spend their money on now and later.

Short term means soon, like a few weeks or months. Short-term savings goals might be a music download, new sneakers, a t-shirt, or movie tickets.

Long-term saving goals span several months to several years. They might not even have a "want" or "need" item attached to them—only an amount. Examples of things you might identify for long-term savings include a fund for emergencies, a bike, a computer, a trip, or a car.

People save by creating a habit that each time money is received, a portion of it is set aside. For example, $2.00 out of every $6.00 allowance.

You set the minimum and go from there. Pay yourself first and then decide what you want to do with the rest.

Do you have anything you have to pay for on a regular basis? This is called a fixed expense. What kinds of fixed expenses do you have? Can you think of any unexpected expenses that have come up for you in the past? Can you think of any you might have now or in the near future?

_____

_____

_____

_____

Okay, so you've got needs, wants, saving goals, and expenses. How do you know if your money will cover all of it? The best way is to keep track of the flow of your cash. This means writing down every amount that comes in and that you pay out and recording the date so you know you can plan if you have enough for an expected expense.

Start by writing down how much money you have. That's called your balance. Then make a column for the money that comes in, deposits and one for money that goes out, withdrawals. Add a column for the date. You can keep track of this/your money by subtracting and adding from and to the balance and describing the purchase or source of income.

It can look like this:

DATE	DESCRIPTION	DEPOSIT	WITHDRAWAL	BALANCE
				20.00
June 1	Birthday gift	20.00		40.00
June 3	Money to savings		10.00	30.00
June 8	Pizza after school		15.00	15.00
June 9	Allowance	8.00		23.00
June 9	Money to savings		3.00	20.00

You can have a separate one for savings that will mostly have deposits.

DATE	DESCRIPTION	DEPOSIT	WITHDRAWAL	BALANCE
				0
June 3	Part of bday gift	10.00		10.00
June 9	Part of allowance	3.00		13.00

CREATE A BUDGET AND MAKE A SAVINGS PLAN

When you get used to keeping track of your money, you can expand and create a budget. That means you can plan on what is going to come in and go out.

If you're serious about saving enough money for some bigger-ticket items, it will help if you create a saving plan by writing the prices and how you will save (time and amounts) for those items.

Most importantly, remember that making and managing your own money will give you lots of pride and self-confidence.

How can you use your savings to help (yourself) achieve your Dreams?

_____

_____

_____

Don't forget to visit PBSKids.org and check out all their online information and money-managing exercises!
http://pbskids.org/itsmylife/money/managing/index.html

Profiles of Success

Mark Cuban is an American business magnate. He is the owner of the National Basketball Association's (NBA) Dallas Mavericks, Landmark Theatres and Magnolia Pictures, and the chairman of the HDTV cable network AXS TV. He is also one of the "shark" investors on the television series Shark Tank.

In 2011, Cuban wrote an eBook, How to Win at the Sport of Business, in which he shares his life experiences in business and sports.

Cuban was born in Pittsburgh, Pennsylvania, and grew up in an average family. At age twelve, he sold garbage bags to pay for a pair of expensive basketball shoes. Later on, when he was still in school he worked at lots of jobs, including bartender, dancing instructor, and party promoter.

Rather than attending high school for his senior year, he enrolled as a full-time student at the University and he transferred to other schools when he found less expensive tuition on the top ten recommended list. He graduated from the Kelley School of Business in 1981 with a bachelor's degree in Business Administration. While he was a student, he purchased a college hangout and called it Motley's Pub. He always invested and saved money. He generated money in creative ways.

"The only thing any entrepreneur, salesperson, or anyone in any position can control is their effort."
Mark Cuban, Businessman

THE GOLDEN RULE
PART ONE OF THREE

Ancient cultures practiced what we universally call: The Golden Rule.

The Golden Rule is about an honorable code of conduct.

The Golden Rule states to treat others as you would like to be treated.

"If you want to have friends, be friendly, if you want to be loved, be loveable. If you want to be wealthy, provide service."
Bob Proctor, Author

Dream Training is all about creating and being the best YOU you can be. None of our Dreams will be successful if we do not follow The Golden Rule.

"Every act rewards itself."
Ralph Waldo Emerson, Philosopher

What are YOU putting out into the Universe?
Are you sending out good thoughts?

Take a moment to evaluate yourself. How do I treat my family?

_____

_____

What about my friends? How do I treat them?

_____

_____

My teachers and coaches?

_____

_____

How do I behave toward my community?

_____

_____

What about the way I interact with this planet?

_____

_____

How can I improve my intentions and interactions?

_____

_____

_____

Acts of giving are essential to success. Think about all the times you have benefitted when someone gave something to you.

Add this affirmation to each day: **Today I give my best to everyone.**

"Those old adages — you attract more with honey; do unto others — are true. You can get attention by being acerbic or mean or making a bizarre

comment. But by being nice, being empathetic, building relationships and listening, people begin to recognize that you're thoughtful and respectful of their position."
Shelley Moore Capito, Politician

Action Beyond Words

What are some ways that you can be of service in your community? Try one of these, or come up with your own.

- Volunteer to help out at your local SPCA or humane society.
- Grab a trash bag and collect any scattered trash around your neighborhood.
- Participate in a recycling program. Or maybe start one.
- Contact your local charities to see if they need help.

What else can you do?

_____

_____

_____

CHAPTER EIGHTEEN

THE GOLDEN RULE
PART TWO OF THREE

On December 30, 1984 LeBron James was born into a family who did not have much money. The family moved a lot when LeBron was young. The family situation was so unstable that, in the fourth grade, LeBron missed eighty-seven days of school.

Fortunately there was a basketball and football coach named Frank Walker, Sr. He arranged for LeBron to live with him in fifth grade. LeBron attended every day of grade five. He went from missing eighty-seven days of school in grade four to ZERO days in grade five. "It was like a new beginning for me," said LeBron.

LeBron became involved in organized sports. He was so eager to learn and improve that his coach made LeBron the assistant coach of the fourth grade team. LeBron realized that everything he did was important. He valued every experience, whether in the gym or at home or in the classroom.

LeBron said, *"Anybody who knows about Elizabeth Park knows how bad it is. You had gunshots flying and cop cars driving around there all the time. As a young boy, it was scary but I never got into none of that stuff. That just wasn't me...I knew it was wrong."*

When LeBron was in high school, he returned to Elizabeth Park and gave out school supplies to the young children. He said he loved seeing the faces of the children as they received their crayons, pens, pencils, and backpacks.

"My achievements in basketball have made me famous, but if I didn't do the work in the classroom you would never know who I am."
LeBron James, Athlete

It could have been very easy for LeBron to give in to the pressures and temptations that existed in the Elizabeth Park community (you might hear these communities referred to as "projects"). LeBron has said he felt secure, even though they moved a lot and he missed school because his mother and extended family showed him so much love. He did not have to seek attention elsewhere—like with older boys involved in illegal activities. He was comfortable being with other kids when they were involved in sports.

THE GOLDEN RULE
PART THREE OF THREE

Would you like to create your own Golden Rulebook? Would you like to use this one, or change it to make it personal?
Think about what goodness and kindness means to you. Think about the Dream/Dreams you've written in this book.

"The future I'm living now, Is not what I thought it would be. The person I was before, Is nothing like me. The future I'm living now, Is the way that I want it to be."
Sick Puppies, Rock Band

Consider signing and dating the contract below. It will give strength to your commitment, and it will be interesting to look back and see the early stages when you learned about Dream Training and made a plan.

MY GOLDEN RULES

1) I will always treat others as I would like to be treated.

2) I will be honest. Honesty builds strength in me, and is fair to others.

3) I will forgive those whom I believe have hurt me because it will bring peace.

4) I will be kind always, without expecting that my kindness will be noticed.

5) I will not say bad things about anyone. Speaking that way is destructive.

6) I will be helpful whenever I can.

_____   _____

Signed   Date

"*Let's take a moment and break the ice, so my intentions are known, see I have pity in watching you suffer, I know the feeling of being damned alone, I've got a storybook all my own.*"
Avenged Sevenfold, Rock Band

ABOUT THE AUTHOR

To say that this book of Dreams grew out of many temporary defeats is an understatement.

Colin Gilmartin grew up in New Hampshire where his parents tried their best to
provide for him and his two younger brothers. Colin readily admits that he was an average student who did the minimum to get by. His passion was playing sports, and he began rec league soccer at age six.

He took his first drink at age twelve and made increasingly poor choices thereafter.
Suspended during his high school senior year for drunkenness, he managed to graduate and begin classes at St. Anselm College, but finished his first year on academic probation. His parents refused to pay for another semester of partying.

On December 8th, 1989, at age nineteen, Colin hit rock bottom after racking up ten felony charges in eight months. He recalls his father's words, "You're a loser, and you're a scum bag, and you're going to prison."

Over the next two weeks, Colin attempted to drink his life away, considering death an option to prison. Then shortly before Christmas, he made a decision to crawl out of the hole he'd dug. He took his last drink on December 23rd, 1989.

Desperate to face his own fears, Colin signed himself into *Straight Incorporated*, a long-term treatment center, on January 4th, 1990. As the fog cleared, he realized he wanted to do three things: get his license back, return to school, and play soccer.

Colin's sixteen months at *Straight* were followed by four months of *Shock Incarceration*, a tough boot camp for first-time, nonviolent offenders. This was Colin's first introduction to Napoleon Hill's philosophy of individual achievement.

The day Colin left *Shock Incarceration*, he returned to St. Anselm's and rejoined the sport he loved—soccer. He majored in psychology to understand himself better, then switched to criminal justice to study and connect him to the legal side of his previous experiences.

Injuries sidelined his soccer playing during his senior year, and Colin began coaching at age twenty-three. He began with the junior varsity team at his former high school. He remembers, *"These kids were willing to do anything I asked because they knew that I cared. They knew their purpose and what I was preparing them for. They were aware I'd been exactly where they were, and that I wanted to help."*

Colin graduated from St. Anselm College in 1994 with a B.S. in Criminal Justice.
He knew he couldn't get a regular job with his criminal record, so he focused on improving his coaching skills. *"Coaching soccer was the vehicle for me to give hope and an opportunity to people that were coming in after me. That was the start of it."*

His first full-time coaching job began in 1997, in Cedar Rapids, Iowa, but wherever he achieved success, jealous rivals brought up his past misdeeds to derail him. After his history followed him to several states, Gilmartin made the decision to tell his students' parents before rumors could start. Astonishingly, they took it well. Colin's criminal record was officially cleared in 2004.

An incredible chain of events brought Colin to Louisiana in 2008. Gilmartin developed a close online friendship with an amazing soul, Ashley Nicole Perrin. Shortly before they could meet, Ashley died in a car accident. Devastated, Colin agreed to meet her family after they learned about him through her journal.

Soon after, Colin accepted a coaching job in southern Louisiana, and moved his life in order to help Ashley's family and her daughter. In the months following Ashley's death, powerful things began to happen. Colin further researched the teachings of Napoleon Hill, Bob Proctor, and others. He was introduced to the music of Avenged Sevenfold and discovered the gifts Ashley had left behind for him.

Witnessing the fear and poor self-esteem in the kids he coached, combined with the expectations of mediocrity from their own parents, Colin knew he had to do more. His search for the tools to help children came up empty; even the Napoleon Hill Foundation had nothing available for children.

In summer of 2011, Colin began writing, determined to gather the best information he could for his students so that they could learn to differentiate between truth, fiction, and opinion, and find their own Greatness. In March 2012, he published Dream Training, a culmination of twenty years of gathering and classifying the best resources he could find. He continued to improve his publication and today a third edition, with its breakthrough in clarity and energy, inspires a generation of young people to recognize the power of their own minds and to do incredible things with it.

"If everyone took the time to inspire a child, the world would have a lot more joy."
Ashley Nicole Perrin

ACKNOWLEDGMENTS

Acknowledgement is the friendly cousin of gratitude; it literarily overflows the page as it pours from my heart. This mission would not be possible without those who have helped me mature.

To the Gilmartins, old and young,
Your every breath supports my own.
Here's to the future, and the newest one: Karol Brandt Gilmartin.

Kudos, Jesse Krieger:
Your can do attitude on the subject of publishing is over the top.

Deep appreciation, Jessica "Ed" Edwards,
for countless hours of research and editing DT2

Cheers, Tom "2 Tall" Cunningham,
Journey to Success Radio,
and everyone at the Napoleon Hill Foundation
for inspiring me to bring big ideas to a new generation.

NODS, WAVES, AND NAMASTES

Sarah Ostlund: the voice of wisdom and reason in youth education.
Leslie Barnes: your name is synonymous for belief in others (including me).
Wendy Dorsey Grossman: unending support is your middle name.
Bob Proctor: mega-talented; your ability to simplify concepts is golden.

Pure Joy, Joy, Joy for the J's:
John Rebstock
Johnny 'Mad Dog' Fedash
Jeff Tipping
Jape Shattuck

And more Love:
Lisa Driscoll

Christine Needler
Maura Barbato

Two soccer visionaries:
Graham Ramsay: one of the finest soccer educators in the world.
Ed Cannon: My college coach who believed in me when no one else would or could.

Personalities, Icons, Families:
Krystal @ Bikram Yoga New Orleans ~ Straight, Inc. ~ Shock Platoon 015 ~ Avenged Sevenfold ~ Otherwise ~ Napoleon Hill ~ Abraham Lincoln ~ Ralph Waldo Emerson ~ Booker T Washington ~ Andrew Carnegie ~ Jackie Robinson ~ Henry Ford ~ Corey Taylor ~ Thomas Edison ~ Jones ~ Higginson ~ Yossi ~ Guven ~ Sinopoli ~ Cambre ~ Penton ~ Santos ~ Quiros ~ Perrin ~The City of New Orleans

I'm unsure if the manuscript was pried or spirited from my hands, but it was rewritten and moved to its final stage by Marie Beswick-Arthur. In order to place her on this page she insists that I say that any errors are hers, not mine. An extra special hug to you, Marie —my editor and writing coach—for rising to the challenge and performing magic.

We are all children.
This book is for every child of every age.
Represented here by the 11 year-old-girls' soccer team of Hammond who generously allow me to be their coach.

Kiley, Delaney, Alaina, Isabella, Sophie, Sage, Lainie, Beth, and Destiny:
You are strong, confident, and powerful individuals.
You possess the qualities to be the best soccer players,
and outstanding citizens.
Your individual belief in yourself is a tower of strength,
permitting no one to interfere with achieving your dreams.
Team affirmation:
"It only takes one person to change your life"

This edition is dedicated to **Adagan Patrick**

The philosophy, spirit, and love that continues to be known as

Ashley Nicole Perrin

Lives on in this book.

Made in the USA
San Bernardino, CA
06 November 2015